What Every Employer
Should Be Doing About
SEXUAL
HARASSMENT

What Every Employer Should Be Doing About SEXUAL HARASSMENT

Susan M. Omilian

BUSINESS & LEGAL REPORTS

BUREAU OF LAW & BUSINESS, INC. • HAZARDOUS WASTE BULLETIN

64 WALL STREET, MADISON, CT 06443-1513

EDITORIAL STAFF:

Editorial Director: Stephen D. Bruce, Ph.D.
Executive Editor: Robert L. Brady, J.D.
Managing Editor: Frank R. Abate
Editorial Associate: Gillian M. Akel
Editorial Assistants: Gillian M. Akel, Jo-Ann P. Milici

DESIGN STAFF:

Art Director: John F. Kallio
Assistant: Kelly Jean Heery

© 1986 BUSINESS & LEGAL REPORTS

First Printing, November 1986

All rights reserved. This book may not be reproduced in part or in whole by any process without written permission from the publisher.

ISBN 1-55645-443-0

Printed in the United States of America

About the author

Susan M. Omilian is an attorney and writer. She is a consultant to employers, including universities and schools, on how to develop internal grievance procedures for sexual harassment complaints. She has written and spoken extensively about sexual harassment in the workplace, on campuses and in housing. As former staff attorney with the Connecticut Women's Educational and Legal Fund, she dealt with issues involving sex discrimination in the workplace.

She holds a bachelor of arts degree from the University of Michigan, and a law degree from Wayne State University Law School in Detroit, Michigan. She is a member of the bar of the states of Connecticut and Michigan and of the U. S. District Courts in Connecticut and Michigan.

Table of Contents

CHAPTER 1. What Is Sexual Harassment? 1
It can happen here ... What can we do? ... What is sexual harassment? ... EEOC guidelines ... Two basic problems ... Puritanical in a liberated age? ... Male and female views ... Victim's perception ... Job related

CHAPTER 2. What Is Your Responsibility for Sexual Harassment? 17
Why the employer is the defendent ... Knowledge ... Other factors ... EEOC rules ... Examples of employer liability

CHAPTER 3. What You Can Do about Sexual Harassment 29
Management's response ... Develop your policy ... Set up your complaint procedure ... Encourage complaints ... Who should handle complaints ... How to handle complaints ... When you find harassment ... Training

CHAPTER 4. What Lies Ahead? 43
How cases are litigated ... An increase in complaints ... Job detriment ... Homosexual harassment ... Other legal patterns

APPENDIX A. BLR Sexual Harassment Survey 49

APPENDIX B. Sample Policies and Forms 69

APPENDIX C. Sample Training Program 83

APPENDIX D. Federal Guidelines Regarding Sexual Harassment 117

Chapter 1

What Is Sexual Harassment?

> **Help Wanted:**
>
> Supervisor seeks subordinate to type, file, and answer telephone. Other job duties include acceptance, without complaint, of the sexual advances of the boss.

Chances are that you have never seen the above advertisement in the classified section of your newspaper—not even prior to 1976, the year when several federal courts found that sexual harassment was illegal sex discrimination in violation of Title VII of the Civil Rights Act of 1964.

Victims of sexual harassment allege that the problem is not that employers are publicly blatant about the existence of sexual harassment. Quite the contrary; sexual harassment is still shrouded in silence. But victims, who are now coming forward with complaints, and employers, who are beginning to act to prevent it in the workplace, are breaking the silent, social acceptance of sexual harassment.

The reality of sexual harassment is that behavior such as that described in the above fictitious advertisement constitutes illegal and disruptive conduct in any workplace.

Yet employers find that dealing with this reality means more than simply wishing it would stop. Instead, employers face the difficult task of developing employment practices that effectively and responsibly combat sexual harassment.

Even if they are aware of the plight of the victim, employers must translate sensitivity into immediate and fair responses to complaints of sexual harassment. Moreover, employers must develop programs and policies to actively prevent sexual harassment. This means an open, frank discussion of its illegality and inappropriateness in the workplace—and its cost to a business organization in lower productivity and employee morale.

This book will help you, the employer, to meet this important challenge. Start with the realization that sexual harassment can happen in *your* workplace.

Sexual Harassment: It Can Happen Anywhere

Some studies have found that sexual harassment is pervasive no matter what the structure or size of the workplace. A 1981 study of the federal workplace by the U.S. Merit Systems Protection Board (MSPB) found that 42 percent of all female and 15 percent of all male employees reported being subjected to sexual harassment. Studies by the Center for Women's Policy Studies in Washington, D.C., have concluded that this rate of sexual harassment is as great or greater in the private sector, although its actual rate may vary from business to business or department to department. For example, the MSPB study suggested that women who work in nontraditional jobs—blue-collar, police, firefighters, building trades or skilled labor—are more likely to be harassed even though, to date, more of the employees who have reported being subjected to sexual harassment hold jobs in traditional fields for women—secretarial, clerical or service occupations.

Furthermore, looking at some of the facts about sexual harassment that emerged from the MSPB study, it is clear that it could happen anywhere.

> FACT #1: Sexual harassment is not motivated merely by sexual desires; it is an abuse of power. Supervisors are harassers in 35 percent of incidents and they are involved in 51 percent of actual or attempted rapes and 44 percent of severe forms of sexual harassment.
>
> FACT #2: Most male and female victims are sexually harassed by persons of the opposite sex who are married and older than the victim.
>
> FACT #3: Harassers act alone in 81 percent of incidents.
>
> FACT #4: Harassers are likely to be repeat offenders—43 percent of victims knew their harasser had bothered others.
>
> FACT #5: Sexual harassment is widely distributed among women and men of various backgrounds, positions and locations.

These facts about sexual harassment and the likelihood that such complaints, if not handled properly, can lead to litigation, should put employers on notice that sexual harassment is an important equal employment issue in the workplace. Furthermore, sexual harassment is costly to any business organization for several reasons.

1. *Litigation costs money*! Attorney's fees, settlements and judgment awards add up. An employer also loses money because of time off by employees to defend lawsuits.

2. *Replacement of employees costs money*! If employees quit because of sexual harassment or are fired because they refuse to acquiesce to sexual demands, valuable on-the-job training is lost. Productivity is lowered when employee turnover is high.

3. *Payment of company benefits is costly*! Absence and tardiness may increase as harassed employees try to avoid an unpleasant situation in the workplace. Employees subjected to sexual harassment may take sick time or disability leave because of the stress that sexual harassment causes them. Also, employees have been filing workers compensation claims for stress-related injuries caused by sexual harassment.

4. *Publicity is damaging!* A single, highly publicized charge can have enormous impact, damaging both employee morale and community support.

5. *Harassment is disruptive!* Even if not discovered, it is causing problems and disrupting productivity.

Nearly two out of three executives, both male and female, said that sexual harassment was bad for business in a 1981 joint survey of 2,000 executives by the *Harvard Business Review* and *Redbook* magazines. These executives believe that it could hurt efficiency by "distracting people and causing dissension." The MSPB study estimates that the cost of sexual harassment in the federal government was over 100 million dollars in a two-year period. These costs are broken down as:

—$22.5 million = JOB TURNOVER (costs of offering job to new employee including background checks and training)

—$3.9 million = EMOTIONAL STRESS (use of health benefits)

—$70.3 million = PRODUCTIVITY (individual and work group)

—$5.3 million = ABSENTEEISM

What can you do about sexual harassment? How can you avoid costly litigation, unnecessary job transition and payment of company benefits to employees subjected to sexual harassment? You, as an employer, can do a lot. Most victims and supervisors in the MSPB study reported that management could do *much* to stop sexual harassment.

What Can You Do?

Sexual harassment is a problem that you can do something about — and relatively easily. Nearly everyone in the workplace will support and applaud your efforts.

A three-step approach to combat sexual harassment is recommended in this book. Each step will be looked at in more detail later. But take a look at the list now and see where you stand.

1. YOU MUST BE SENSITIVE.

    You and your entire managment team can learn about sexual harassment. Sexual harassment has many definitions, but it has been defined. Sexual harassment has many consequences—for the individual victim and for the organization—which can be recognized. Sexual harassment can be prevented if you look at some of the reasons why it exists and why it has been grudgingly tolerated in the past. With this knowledge of sexual harassment, comes a sensitivity to its victims and the potential ability to deal with it effectively.

2. YOU MUST BE RESPONSIVE.

    You can set up a system to respond immediately and fairly to complaints of sexual harassment in your workplace. The system will *not* encourage frivolous or unfounded complaints. It will give your employees a trusted, credible source, *within* the company, to talk about concerns and get some action. First, the company should set up a policy against sexual harassment so that employees know it is not a joking matttter and that if they have complaints, they will be taken seriously by top management. Secondly, a consistent and fair internal grievance procedure should be instituted that allows for a thorough and objective investigation of *all* complaints of sexual harasssment.

3. YOU MUST BE ACTIVE.

    You should train *every* employee in your company about sexual harassment concerns. Train your hourly employees to understand not only that sexual harassment is against company policy but also that they can complain without fear of retaliation. Train supervisors to handle complaints of sexual harassment sensitively and judiciously. Train top management to be consistent and fair in disciplining *any* employee at *any* management level who has been found, after a thorough investigation, to have sexually harassed an employee or employees. Finally, integrate the issue of sexual harassment into your equal opportunity program at all levels so that awareness of sexual harassment and action to prevent it in your workplace is ongoing.

With a sensitive approach, an immediate response and an active program, your company can effectively combat sexual harassment. It has worked for other companies and for individual victims of sexual harassment. In the chapters to come, we will relate some of the success stories and point out some of the ways a company could have acted in a given situation. Begin by knowing that sexual harassment can happen in *your* workplace and that there are ways to fight against it if you are willing to meet the challenge.

WHAT IS SEXUAL HARASSMENT?

Probably the toughest question you will ask yourself as you study sexual harassment is—"what is it?" You wonder: Can it be defined? What kind of behavior are we talking about? What is illegal about sexual harassment and why? That answer lies first in what women have experienced in the workplace, not only today but long before the term "sexual harassment" was coined. Here are some examples:

—An 1864 report to the U. S. Congress documents how a young woman working in the U.S. Printing Bureau could be seduced by a male supervisor who "surrounded her with flattery, temptations of every description, and when these failed, threatened her with dismissal from the place which she earns her bread, if she does not yield." (Dr. John Ellis, *The Sights and Secrets of the National Capitol,* U. S. Publishing Co., 1869, p. 385)

—In 1976, more than 9,000 people responded to a readership survey in *Redbook* magazine. Nearly half of them reported that they, or someone they knew, had quit a job or been fired because of sexual harassment. They documented that sexual harassment on the job included:

1. "Sexual remarks — by far the most frequent form of interchange — can be anything from a passing comment on a woman's legs to the experience of an 18-year-old file clerk whose boss regularly called her into his office to 'tell me the intimate details of his marriage and to ask what I thought about different sexual positions.'"

2. "Touching (which) can be the bumping of bodies at the water cooler with those unsettling doubts about whether it was 'accidental,' or it can be the unmistakable hand where it clearly doesn't belong."

The *Redbook* survey further found that the visual (leering, ogling) and verbal (sexual remarks or teasing) abuse of women can easily "escalate to pinching, grabbing and touching to subtle hints and pressures to overt requests for dates and sexual favors — with the implied threat that it will go against the woman if she refuses."

In the 1981 MSPB study of the federal workplace, a majority of the women identified all six of these behaviors to be sexual harassment.

1. Uninvited pressure for sexual favors,

2. Uninvited and deliberate touching, leaning over, cornering or pinching,

3. Uninvited sexually suggestive looks or gestures,

4. Uninvited letters, phone calls or materials of a sexual nature,

5. Uninvited pressure for dates, and,

6. Uninvited sexual teasing, jokes, remarks or questions.

The study also found that these acts of sexual harassment were repeated—most going on for a week, and a sizeable percentage lasting for more than six months. In addition, one percent of federal employees surveyed reported being subjected to the most severe forms of sexual harassment—attempted sexual assault or an actual sexual assault. Although a small percentage, it is a significant number considering: 1) the seriousness of these actions and 2) that they are criminal offenses.

Other research has uncovered a more subtle and undermining category of sexual harassment—what Dr. Mary Rowe of the Massachusetts Institute of Technology has coined "microinequities." Dr. Rowe, who, as Special Assistant to the President of MIT, has mediated hundreds of harassment cases since 1974, finds, in her experience, that these "microinequities" usually are not actionable. She writes: "Most are such petty incidents that they may not even be identified (as discrimination), much less protected." Yet she compares them to the "dust and ice in Saturn's rings, because taken together they constitute formidable barriers. As Saturn is partially obscured by its rings, so are good jobs (for women) partially obscured by [grains of sand] the minutiae of discrimination."

Dr. Karen Bogart has, in her research on sexual harassment through the American Institute for Research, built on this idea of "microinequities" and classified the following as some of the more subtle forms of sex discrimination women face in the workplace: (Dr. Bogart's research focuses on women students and teachers in postsecondary education institutions.)

Condescension—refusing to take women seriously.

Sexist comments—making derogatory remarks about women's inferiority, frivolousness, emotionalism.

Exclusion—Unintentionally or deliberately overlooking women and denying them access to places or people where information for upper mobility may be informally exchanged.

Tokenism—the discretionary inclusion of one or only a few women.

(Taken from an article, "Sexual Harassment of Women in Employment Part II: Promising Solutions," by Jane Roberts Chapman and Gordon R. Chapman in *Response*, Fall, 1984.)

According to the Working Women United Institute (WWUI) in New York, the underlying assumption in all these behaviors is that a woman's existence as a sexual being is more important than her work. Indeed, a common thread is the sexual nature of all this conduct. Yet a more accurate description of the similarity is that all of these behaviors are about the power some employees have over other employees. That is, the inappropriate sexual behavior is only the *way* or *method* by which individual employees abuse their power.

The most obvious example is when a supervisor, who has the power to hire, fire, promote or offer other job benefits to a subordinate, conditions use of that power on a subordinate's willingness to accede to sexual advances. The classic case is the use of a demand/threat like: "Either you go out with me or I'll fire you." The power imbalance is clear; the goodwill of a supervisor is the key to a subordinate's further advancement in a job (a promotion or good reference) or future employment (discharge, demotion, layoff). In that case, the subordinate has two choices: submit and hope that the personal relationship will save the job (but there is no guarantee) or refuse and hope that the supervisor will not carry out the threat.

Lin Farley, author of *Sexual Shakedown: The Sexual Harassment of Women on the Job (McGraw Hill, N.Y. 1978)*, labels this kind of sexual harassment as the way in which women are "kept down" in their jobs — particularly in the traditional female occupations of clerical, service or retail.

But co-workers can also exercise a certain amount of control over fellow employees, and in the sexual harassment arena, this power imbalance is most often seen in nontraditional jobs for women, such as the skilled trades, factory work, police or fire officers. Male co-workers — usually a group of men against one or a few women — can use inappropriate sexual conduct to "keep women out" of these jobs. Sexual abuse by male co-workers, particularly if unchecked by management, will make it so difficult for the female worker to perform her job that she may quit rather than put up with it.

Here are a few examples of co-worker sexual harassment from recent court cases:

—Initially, a female worker, who was one of only two women employed in a warehouse, got along fine with her male co-workers. But then one male co-worker asked her on several different occasions if she was wearing a bra. When this co-worker was not seriously reprimanded for his comments, others joined in. Over the next three years, one male co-worker exposed his buttocks to the plaintiff 10-20 times. Others also exposed their buttocks, made crude sexual remarks and called the plaintiff by offensive, abusive and derogatory names for women. Some male co-workers began posting drawings, many depicting naked women with exaggerated sexual features and some with the plaintiff's initials on them. While the female worker complained frequently to her supervisors, management did not effectively act to stop this abusive conduct. The Wisconsin federal district court found the company liable for co-workers' acts which created a hostile, offensive and intimidating working environment for the plaintiff (*Zabkowicz v. West Bend Co.*, 35 FEP Cases 611 (D. Wisc. 1974)).

—The only female on a crew of federal air traffic controllers was subjected to sexual harassment in a workplace which the federal appellate court in Richmond, Virginia, (Fourth Circuit) determined was "pervaded with sexual slurs, insults, innuendoes."

The court concluded that she was the object of "sustained, nontrivial" sexual harassment by her co-workers which her supervisors failed to stop and in which, in fact, some participated. It ruled that the company was liable (*Katz v. Dole*, 31 FEP Cases 1521 (4th Cir. 1983)).

In these cases, the male co-workers, because they outnumbered the females and were unchecked in their behavior by their supervisors, had power over the female workers. They exercised that power with the most effective weapon they had—abusive sexual misconduct—to make the females feel uncomfortable and unsafe in their workplaces.

From all of the above documentation, the experiences which women have labeled as sexual harassment can be broadly defined as "...any unwanted attention of a sexual nature that occurs in the process of working or seeking work and jeopardizes a person's ability to earn a living." This definition, taken from a booklet entitled *Sexual Harassment on the Job: A Guide for Employers*, published by the Massachusetts Advisory Committee to the U.S. Commission on Civil Rights, presents a "behavioral" model for sexual harassment. That is, it generalizes a definition of sexual harassment from all the specific behaviors that have been identified in the research above as sexual harassment.

While it does not address which of these behaviors might be actionable in a court of law, this behavioral model does help pinpoint characteristics about sexual harassment that would most likely make it illegal—notably under Title VII of the Civil Rights Act of 1964, the federal law that outlaws employment discrimination on the basis of such factors as race, sex, religion and national origin. For example, in describing the more blatant kinds of sexual harassment (such as sexual remarks, requests for sexual favors or touching), the behavioral model identifies two key factors—it is *unwelcomed* and there is a *job-related* threat if the employee does not go along. These factors recognize that "flirtation" or "sexual play" on the job becomes sexual harassment when it goes beyond the joking stage to become offensive, humiliating or uncomfortable, or it results in someone losing his or her job or a long-awaited promotion.

EEOC Guidelines

Let's look at how these two factors—"unwanted sexual attention" and "job-relatedness"—fit into a legal definition of sexual harassment. Title VII, when it was passed in 1964, did not specifically define sexual harassment. It was not until 1980 that the Equal Employment Opportunity Commission (EEOC), the federal agency which enforces antidiscrimination laws, formulated its guidelines on sexual harassment. Although they do not have the force of law, the guidelines set forth the EEOC's interpretation of how sexual harassment is illegal sex discrimination under Title VII. (A complete text of these regulations is included in the appendix to this book.) Let's look at some of the key concepts covered in the EEOC guidelines.

—"Sexual harassment is any *unwelcomed* sexual advances, requests for sexual favors and other verbal or physical conduct of a sexual nature."

—It occurs when:

1. Sexual favors are demanded "as a term or condition of employment." *Example*: A supervisor demands that a subordinate employee sleep with him or she will be fired.

2. Sexual demands, once made, are refused and the employee faces an adverse consequence for that refusal. *Example*: An employee rejects the sexual advance of her boss and she is demoted and later fired for her refusal.

3. The acts of verbal abuse, physical touching, sexual demands or other conduct of a sexual nature are so pervasive and persistent as to have "the effect of unreasonably interfering with an individual's work performance or creating an offensive and intimidating working environment " for an employee. *Example*: Male employees tease and insult women in the workplace with obscene jokes, sexual innuendoes or displays of pinup girl posters. The female employees are embarrassed and offended by this behavior which is carried out by co-workers with supervisors doing little to stop it, or by the supervisors themselves with top management doing nothing.

—The relationship of the harasser to the harassed employee may be supervisor to subordinate, co-worker to co-worker, or nonemployee (such as a business visitor or customer) to an employee on the job. In all of these situations, the employer has the ability to stop the sexual harassment.

Two Basic Problems

Thus the EEOC guidelines establish a legal cause of action for sexual harassment when it occurs in two basic fact patterns. One is the *quid pro quo*, or "job detriment" case in which a sexual demand is made in exchange for something else ("If you sleep with me, I'll give you a promotion.") and if there is a refusal of the sexual demand, the employee faces an adverse consequence ("Since you will not sleep with me, you are fired."). The second is when the sexual harassment creates a "hostile working environment." An example is the co-worker harassment described above.

The guidelines are clear that a legal cause of action does not arise from a "flirtation" or unwelcomed sexual attentions that are not attached in some way to the workplace. In fact, the "microinequities" discussed earlier are probably not actionable under the EEOC guidelines. However, the guidelines do set up the parameters, which are consistent with Title VII principles, for actionable sexual harassment cases that do include most of the kinds of behavior workers have labeled as sexual harassment in the workplace.

Federal courts across the country, including the U.S. Supreme Court, have now not only generally endorsed the EEOC guidelines on sexual harassment, but also have recognized a legal cause of action for sexual harassment under Title VII since 1976. The most recent pronouncement was by the U.S. Supreme Court in *Meritor Savings Bank,*

FSB. v. Mechelle Vinson, 54 U.S. Law Week 4703, (June 19, 1986) *sub nom Vinson v. Taylor,* 36 FEP Cases 1423 (D.C. Cir. 1985); 23 FEP Cases 37 (D.D.C. 1980). Justice William H. Rehnquist wrote for the Court: "When a supervisor sexually harasses a subordinate because of a subordinate's sex, that supervisor discriminates on the basis of sex." Many courts, in fact, now agree on what facts a plaintiff must prove in order to win a sexual harassment case. Proof of these essential facts at trial establishes what is known legally as a *prima facie* case. Not surprisingly, two of the facts that the plaintiff must prove are:

1. She was subjected to unwelcomed sexual harassment (sexual advances, requests for sexual favors or other verbal or physical conduct of a sexual nature,

2. The harassment complained of affected a term or condition or privilege of employment.

[*Henson v. City of Dundee,* 29 FEP Cases 787 (11th Cir. 1982)]

Now we have answered, at least theoretically, what sexual harassment is. We have identified a behavioral model, a legal definition and some elements of the *prima facie* case of sexual harassment. But some more pragmatic concerns remain. Where is the line between sexual harassment and flirtation? What if the harasser did not mean to harass by that conduct? How is sexual harassment related to the workplace?

The answers to these questions may be found by looking more carefully at each of the elements we have determined above to be important characteristics of sexual harassment.

Puritanical in a Liberated Age?

Surely what is unwanted by one individual may not be so for another. In fact, sexual "teasing" in the workplace, psychiatrist Carroll Brodsky believes, can be healthy, benign and mutually pleasurable. It is a way to approach sex in the workplace and release tension.

However, she finds that if one party lacks sensitivity, the healthy teasing may escalate into harassment.

> *Harassment is an interaction in which one person purposefully seeks to discomfort the other person. In contrast to teasing, harassment is not mutually satisfactory and is not enjoyable to all persons engaged in it.*
>
> [From "Rape at Work" in Walker, *Sexual Assault,* (Lexington Books, 1976) p. 35.]

While each workplace interaction of a sexual nature cannot be instantly analyzed by looking for mutual pleasure or satisfaction, it is true that men often misread how a woman feels about sexual attentions on the job and assume that she is always flattered or feels complimented. Only 15 percent of women in the *Redbook* magazine survey found verbal or visual sexual attentions or sexual advances to be "flattering." Seventy-five percent of women said that these unwelcome attentions were "embarrassing," "demeaning" and "insulting."

Male and Female Views Differ

Do men and women, then, differ in the point at which "healthy teasing" becomes offensive harassment? Let's look at the MSPB study of the federal workplace for the answer.

—Recall the list of six behaviors that were identified by a majority of the women as sexual harassment, whether initiated by supervisors or co-workers (uninvited pressure for sexual favors, uninvited and deliberate touching, leaning over, cornering or pinching, etc.). The majority of male respondents agreed with the women in this regard, but only if these behaviors were done by a supervisor. They did not consider sexually suggestive looks, gestures, remarks, joking or teasing to be harassment when coming from co-workers.

—Male and female respondents agreed that three behaviors—letters and calls, pressure for sexual favors and deliberate touching—were sexual harassment, whether from co-workers or supervisors. These more overt, flagrant or "severe" (as the survey coined them) forms of sexual harassment were thought to be different than actions which were more subtle or whose meaning and intent was more ambiguous, such as suggestive looks and sexual remarks. The latter forms of sexual harassment were "less severe" and most men found them not to be sexual harassment.

The most obvious observation about this data is that men and women view sexual harassment differently. But it is more complex that that. Women in the MSPB study were more likely than men to be victims of sexual harassment. (Forty-two percent of women but only 15 percent of men reported being sexually harassed.) That means that the majority of men in the survey had never been victims of sexual harassment and some could have been harassers themselves. On the other hand, the majority of women in the survey, who had identified all six forms of behavior as sexual harassment, were very likely to have been victims. Therefore, from a *victim's* point of view, all of these behaviors, even ones whose meanings may have been ambiguous, were more definitely sexual harassment than not.

Victim's Perception Counts

The EEOC guidelines affirm that the victim's perception of sexual harassment is controlling. The guidelines specifically deal with "unwelcomed" sexual conduct when it "has the *effect* of unreasonably interfering with an individual's work performance or creating an intimidating, hostile or offensive work environment." Sexual remarks or touching may be *intended* not to harass, but if those actions have the *effect* of making the recipient feel uncomfortable, humiliated, embarrassed or unsafe in her working environment, they are sexual harassment.

Many commentators have questioned the wisdom of the EEOC's approach, but several federal courts have upheld a standard of proof that sexual harassment is in the subjective perception of the victim. The most important case was *Bundy v. Jackson*, in which the federal appellate court in the District of Columbia focused on the psychological and emotional impact that the unwelcomed sexual attentions had on the victim. The court found that the "sexually stereotyped insults" and "demeaning propositions" she was forced to endure did her "serious emotional harm" and caused her "anxiety and debilitation."

This concern with the state of mind of the sexual harassment victim led the *Bundy* court to hold an employer liable for a workplace which was "poisoned" for her by the unwelcomed sexual behavior, regardless of what the intent of that behavior was. [24 FEP Cases 1155 (D.C. Cir. 1981)]

In *Caldwell v. Hodgeman*, a Massachusetts state court, which was deciding an unemployment compensation case involving a claim of sexual harassment, applauded the *Bundy* court's analysis. That court affirmed that a court should look to the state of mind of the victim of the sexual harassment, not to the intent of the harasser. To bolster this position, the court cited the joint *Harvard Business Review/Redbook* study of 2,000 executives in which, similar to the MSPB study results, women viewed sexual harassment differently from men. There, male executives were unwilling to define "sexual horseplay" and "subtle advances" as clear-cut harassment, while women executives were more likely to think that such behavior could constitute sexual harassment. Given a list of 14 examples of behaviors that could have sexual implications, women executives were twice as likely as men to say they had seen or heard of these on the job.

Other courts have also looked for proof that the sexual attentions were sexual harassment from the victim's point of view. In *Heelan v. Johns-Mansville Inc.*, 451 F.Supp. 1382 (D. Colorado, 1978), the Colorado federal district court determined that because the plaintiff was subjected to many sexual demands from her supervisor over a period of two years, her case constituted the "paradigm of repeated, unwelcomed sexual advances." In *Lamb v. Drilco Div.*, the court considered the fact that the plaintiff's job performance deteriorated, that she was upset and unable to concentrate, eat or sleep, proof that she was subjected to unwanted sexual harassment (32 FEP Cases 105 (S.D. Texas, 1983)). Finally, in *Gan v. Kepro Circuit Systems*, a plaintiff, who complained of a hostile working environment because of unwelcomed sexual harassment, was found not to be the object of such harassment. The evidence showed instead that because she actively contributed to the distasteful working environment by her own profane and sexually suggestive conduct, she failed to prove that her working conditions were personally intolerable (28 FEP Cases 639 (E.D. Missouri, 1982)).

A Definite Line

What are we to make of this? One thing. There is a definite line between flirtation and harassment, and that line is crossed when the victim perceives it to have been crossed. But since the line is not the same for every individual, sexual harassment must be examined on a case-by-case basis. But keep three things in mind:

1. DO NOT ASSUME MUTUALITY IN EVERY CASE

The appearance that some employees are not offended by sexual attentions or remarks can be deceiving. An employee may smile at an off-color joke, laugh when touched in a sexual way or seem to cooperate with requests for sexual favors. But this may be because the employee fears for her job or knows that she must put up with it since a complaint to a supervisor would not be taken seriously. In observing a situation that could, in the victim's perception, be sexual harassment, a manager should ask the employee on the receiving end directly: "Does that offend you?" or "How did what just happened feel?" Let the employee know that a complaint is appropriate and will be acted upon.

2. DO NOT ASSUME THAT THE VICTIM IS BEING TOO "SENSITIVE."

That is not an appropriate response to a sexual harassment complaint. It will not stop the employee from feeling that she is being harassed. It will not stop the alleged harasser who may continue with behavior he or she thinks is nonoffensive. It does not stop the aggrieved employee from filing a lawsuit and letting the judge decide what is sexual harassment and what is not. You must work to understand what is offensive about the behavior for the individual employee and what will make the alleged harasser modify his or her behavior.

3. DO NOT FOCUS ON WHAT THE ALLEGED HARASSER INTENDED BY THE BEHAVIOR.

What the employee who made the sexual remark intended by it may not be the issue. The employee may need to be confronted about intent of this behavior and the effect on the victim, but do not dismiss a complaint of sexual harassment merely because the behavior, in the harasser's mind or yours, did not intend to offend or the allegation was denied by the harasser. Several employers, as will be discussed in a later chapter, made this mistake and were held legally liable for the harassment because they failed to take immediate corrective action.

One company in a recent court case did take action in a complaint that upon investigation they found to be sexual harassment *in the perception of the victim*. They confronted the alleged harasser and let him know that his sexist comments and abusive behavior would not be tolerated. The harassment stopped and when the case was brought to trial, the court fount that the company was not liable because it had taken effective corrective action on a complaint where there was sexual harassment in the victim's perception (*Ferguson v. Dupont,* 31 FEP Cases 795 (D. Delaware 1983)).

Without this focus on the victim's perception of what is sexual harassment, the problem of sexual harassment might never be addressed by an employer. All victims might easily be labeled as "too sensitive" and their complaints dismissed as "exaggerations." This is certainly possible; there are dramatically different perceptions of male and female respondents to what is sexual harassment in the studies cited above.

JOB-RELATED

One respondent in the *Harvard Business Review/Redbook* survey, a 60-year-old female executive, put it this way. "I find a woman must defend herself every day. I had to learn to either say 'no' graciously or lose every good job I got."

But in the 1970s, individual women began to seek a legal remedy for the sexual harassment as a form of illegal sex discrimination in the workplace. For example, in 1973, two female workers brought a lawsuit claiming that they were repeatedly subjected to verbal and physical sexual demands by their supervisors. Unable to stop this behavior, or cope with it day after day, they voluntarily quit their jobs. An Arizona federal district court dismissed their lawsuit even though it found that the actions of the supervisor were "inappropriate behaviors of a sexual nature." Though inappropriate, the court characterized them as "merely the personal proclivity, peculiarity or mannerism" of the supervisor, not related to the "nature of employment" (*Corne v. Bausch & Lomb Inc.*, 10 FEP Cases 289 (D. Ariz, 1975)).

The finding in this 1975 case was overruled on appeal to a higher federal court and contradicted by the 1980 EEOC guidelines. The guidelines state that sexual advances by a supervisor are a term and condition of employment. This was clearly established in *Williams v. Saxbe*, where the court determined that the actions of the supervisor created an "artificial barrier to employment" for women which Congress intended to eradicate with Title VII. These unwelcomed sexual demands were not an isolated personal incident or simply a dispute between employees of no concern to the court (413 F. Supp. 654 (D.D.C. 1976)).

Similarly, several federal courts ruled initially that sexual demands or abuses that did not result in a tangible job detriment fell outside Title VII's scope of discrimination because they did not touch on "terms, conditions or privileges of employment." But in *Bundy v. Jackson,* the federal appellate court in the District of Columbia established the "hostile environment" theory of sexual harassment, endorsing the EEOC guidelines' delineation the previous year of that cause of action. The court found that "conditions of employment" included the "psychological and emotional work environment" which, in this case, was illegally "poisoned" by the sexual harassment the plaintiff endured.

This legal conclusion was built on previous race discrimination cases in which the courts ruled that blacks and other minorities do not have to work in environments "heavily charged with ethnic or racial discrimination" (*Rogers v. EEOC*, 454 F. 2d 234, 4 FEP Cases 92 (5th Cir. 1972)). In *Rogers,* the plaintiff, a Hispanic woman, claimed that her employer, a firm of opticians, had, by giving discriminatory service to its Hispanic clients, created a discriminatory and offensive environment for its Hispanic employees.

The *Bundy* court reasoned that if racial harassment was illegal race discrimination, how then can sexual harassment "which injects the most demeaning sexual stereotypes into the general work environment and which always represents an intentional assault on an individual's innermost privacy," not be illegal sex discrimination?

In June 1986, the U.S. Supreme Court, the highest court in the country, unanimously affirmed this view of sexual harassment as illegal sexual discrimination in *Meritor Savings Bank, FSB. v. Mechelle Vinson*. Vinson alleged that her supervisor made repeated sexual demands of her; he fondled her in front of co-workers, exposed himself to her, followed her into the women's room and forcibly raped her. The Supreme Court found that Vinson's charges, "which not only include pervasive harassment but also criminal conduct of the most serious nature—are plainly sufficient to state a claim for 'hostile environment' sexual harassment" (54 U.S. Law Week at 4706).

Since *Williams, Bundy,* and *Meritor Savings Bank* have now clearly established that sexual harassment is job-related, an employer must realize that what may seem like a personal sexual encounter between two employees may be or could evolve into sexual harassment. An employer cannot regulate all the personal conduct of its employees, and pragmatically, many employers would prefer that their workplace be free of all sexual behaviors, even the mutual ones. To that end, some employers have set "no-dating" policies, but enforcement has to be impossible. What is possible is for an employer's management team to be sensitive as to how mutual sexual encounters can turn into sexual harassment, how an individual's job performance can be affected by unwelcome sexual attentions, and how a victim's perception of sexual harassment needs to be seriously considered.

What Is Sexual Harassment?

It is an illegal form of sex discrimination that recognizes that, but for an employee's gender, he or she would not be subjected to unwelcome sexual attentions. It is an intrusion into an employee's privacy and is a barrier to fair and humane treatment for all employees. Instead of being judged on their job performance, victims of sexual harassment have been denied promotions, lost job benefits or been fired merely because they refused to put up with unwelcome sexual attentions.

Sexual harassment is also a way in which the victims, mostly women, are told that they are not accepted as equals in the workplace. It tells them that all too often they can please some employers by how they look, not what they do on the job.

Employers who are sensitive and willing to combat sexual harassment can create a workplace that recognizes the equality of all its employees and is free of offensive sexual behavior. That goal makes sense, not only because it promotes good employee relations, but also because it helps an employer meet its legal responsibility for the sexual harassment of its workers.

Chapter 2

What Is Your Responsibility for Sexual Harassment?

The court decisions are clear: Employers *are* responsible for conduct that constitutes the sexual harassment of employees in their workplace.

This position, taken by judges across the country since 1976 and by the EEOC in their guidelines on sexual harassment issued in 1980, places the legal liability for sexual harassment of workers squarely on the employer. It also triggers an employer's duty to investigate complaints of sexual harassment.

We'll discuss the investigation stage more in the next chapter. First, let's look at why and how an employer is responsible for the actions of its employees when they sexually harass.

Why the Employer Is the Defendent

In any employment discrimination suit against an employer, the company or corporation will be the "defendents," or the party who is defending against the allegations of the lawsuit. Sometimes, the "plaintiff," or the party bringing the legal action, will also name individual workers who allegedly actually were the harassers. But the employer is really the legal entity that the lawsuit and Title VII of the Civil Rights Act of 1964 is directed at. This is because only the company, and not any individual employee, has the ability to provide the relief that the plaintiff seeks. For example, only the employer can reinstate the plaintiff or give her back pay or other remedies which are authorized in Title VII and may be ordered by the judge.

But beside the fact that the employer holds the key to possible relief for the plaintiff, law has developed over the centuries that clearly puts the responsibility for the acts of an employee onto the employer. This is a legal doctrine called *"respondeat superior."*

In the passage of Title VII, the U.S. Congress adopted an expanded version of *respondeat superior* which casts the employee, in an employment discrimination case, as an "agent" of the employer. What Title VII outlaws the employer from doing, the agent (employee) of that employer is also forbidden to do.

Recently, a federal appellate court in the District of Columbia confirmed this view of the relationship between an employer and its employees who have broad supervisory powers to hire, fire, promote or make other important job decisions. The court wrote:

> *An employer's delegation of this much authority vests in the supervisor such extreme power over the victimized employee that the supervisor's status as an 'agent' of the employer cannot be doubted.*
>
> (*Vinson v. Taylor,* 36 FEP Cases 1423, 1430 (D.C. Cir., 1985) *affirmed in part,* 54 U.S. Law Week 4703 (June 19, 1986).)

The court noted that the mere existence—or even the appearance—of influence over vital job decisions gives any supervisor the opportunity to impose upon employees because such authority carries "the attendant power to coerce and harass."

Many supervisory employees properly exercise their power over subordinates. But when abuses occur, the employer must deal with the supervisor who exceeds his or her authority and in the employment discrimination area, this means monitoring for supervisors who display sexist or racist behavior.

For these reasons, an employer must answer for the harassment of any subordinate by a supervisor. However, we must mention one court case in which the judge was able to fashion another deterrent to sexual harassment. In *Kriazi v. Western Electric*, a New Jersey federal district court judge decided a complex Title VII lawsuit in which the woman plaintiff, an industrial engineer, alleged she was sexually harassed by male co-workers in her department. She also sought "punitive" damages under state tort law against her co-workers. After hearing the trial testimony, the judge concluded that these co-workers had made the plaintiff's work environment "intolerable."

The judge wrote:

> *They shot rubber bands at her. They engaged in boisterous speculations about her virginity. They circulated an obscene cartoon depiction of her.*
>
> [26 FEP Cases 398, 416-417 (D. N.J. 1979)]

Outraged by this behavior, the judge ordered each of the individual co-workers to *personally* pay the plaintiff $1,500 as a punishment for their actions. And he made it clear that the employer could not pay the sum!

HOW AND WHEN THE EMPLOYER IS LIABLE

If the *respondeat superior* principles embodied in Title VII provide "why" an employer is responsible for employees who sexually harass, let's now look at *how and when* an employer can be liable. For example, what if the employer did not know that the harassment was going on? Can it still be held legally liable even without notice?

Before we can answer these questions, we need to examine what is "notice" and how an employer gets knowledge that sexual harassment is occurring in the workplace.

Knowledge

There are two kinds of knowledge that a court will look for in a sexual harassment case:

1. The employee, who is being sexually harassed, tells someone in authority. That may be her supervisor, unless it is her supervisor who is doing the harassing, or someone else in management. This complaint may be through an established employee grievance procedure or informally to someone in the company, such as an EEO officer or a company omsbudperson, if that position exists. If the complaint comes from the victim, the employer would legally have "actual knowledge" of the sexual harassment.

2. The employer may be able, through its managment or EEO team, to observe or sense that sexual harassment is going on. In several cases, the courts have found that the sexual harassment so invaded the workplace that the employer must have known about it. For example, in *Katz v. Dole,* the federal appellate court in Richmond, Virginia (Fourth Circuit), ruled that the employer was or should have been aware of the sexual harassment of the plaintiff, a female air traffic controller, because her workplace was "pervaded with sexual slur, insult and innuendo" and she personally was the object of verbal sexual harassment by fellow controllers. [31 FEP Cases 1521 (4th Cir. 1983)] In another case, which alleged both racial and sexual harassment, the federal appellate court in St. Louis, Missouri (Eighth Circuit), found that knowledge of harassment will be imputed to the employer when the harassment is so "disruptive" of the workplace environment. In this workplace, the court found that the racial atmosphere was "dismal" and that prejudice was so pervasive and long-continuing that the "employer must have become conscious of it" [*Taylor v. Jones,* 28 FEP Cases 1024 (8th Cir. 1981)]. When an employer receives this kind of notice of sexual harassment, it is legally called "constructive knowledge."

Other Factors

Beside the notice an employer has of the sexual harassment, the extent of an employer's liability for employees who harass has to do with the legal definition of sexual harassment. As you recall from the previous chapter, sexual harassment can occur 1) when the employee is put in a position of accepting sexual advances as a condition of employment—a "job detriment" is involved, or, 2) when the conduct creates a "hostile, offensive or intimidating work environment." Furthermore, sexual harassment can occur due to the actions of supervisors, co-workers or even nonemployees.

Employer Liability and "Hostile Environment"

All of the factors mentioned above have been considered by the EEOC and the federal courts in arriving at the following rules about employer liability in sexual harassment cases:

> RULE # 1: AN EMPLOYER IS LEGALLY LIABLE FOR THE SEXUAL HARASSMENT OF ITS EMPLOYEES BY *SUPERVISORY* PERSONNEL EVEN IF IT HAD *NO NOTICE* OF THE ILLEGAL CONDUCT.

The federal courts of appeal in several parts of the country have found that victims of sexual harassment have a cause of action against an employer even if they did not notify the employer of the harassment. That means that it is not a *defense* to a sexual harassment lawsuit that an employer did not know about the illegal conduct.

Why such a strict rule for employer liability? Reflect back on the words of the District of Columbia judge who wrote about the tremendous power an employer gives a supervisor. Think, too, about our earlier discussion of sexual harassment as an abuse of power, not a sexual act.

What the federal courts and the EEOC have established is that this power of a supervisor can be so easily abused that the employer has a special duty of actively monitoring the actions of its supervisory employees. This interpretation of Title VII is the strongest incentive that Congress could give to an employer, in the words once again of the District of Columbia judge, "to take a more active role in warranting to each employee that he or she will enjoy a working environment free from illegal sex discrimination." Legally, this liability without defenses is called "strict liability."

Here's an example of a court ruling upholding the strict liability rule:

—A female factory worker for a mobile home manufacturer alleged she was discharged because she refused the sexual advances of the plant superintendent. She was subjected, she said, to his leers, obscene gestures, lewd comments, remarks about her sexual needs after she separated from her husband and promises that things "would go easy" if she would go out with him. Two weeks after the last refusal, he fired her. Other women employees testified at trial that the superintendent had a fired her. Other women employees testified at trial that the superintendent had a "propensity to sexually exploit women who were vulnerable because of marital problems and financial dependency on their jobs." When she was terminated, she told his superior about the sexual harassment. This manager, after investigating the charges, concluded that the woman was terminated because of her personal problems and not for refusal to submit to sexual demands. The federal appellate court in Chicago, Illinois (Seventh Circuit), disagreed and found that not only did plaintiff's supervisor make sexual advances toward the plaintiff but also he operated so that sexual harassment entered into the "totality" of all his relationships with women in the plant." The court ruled that even though the employer did not have notice of the sexual harassment until after plaintiff was terminated, it was still liable for the acts of its supervisor for the following reasons:

1. These acts of sexual harassment are not personal acts of the supervisor. The company is a legal entity which can act only through its agent/employees.

2. An employer will be held strictly liable to encourage it to take positive steps to prevent the hiring and retention of "sexist" supervisors.

3. Other courts have applied strict liability in every other Title VII employment discrimination context. Sexual harassment should not be the exception.

[*Horn v. Duke Homes,* 37 FEP Cases 228 (7th Cir. 1985)]

RULE #2: AN EMPLOYER MAY NOT BE LIABLE FOR ACTIONS BY ITS SUPERVISORS IF THE ILLEGAL CONDUCT CREATED A "HOSTILE, OFFENSIVE AND INTIMIDATING WORK *ENVIRONMENT" AND* THE EMPLOYER HAD *NO NOTICE* OF THE CONDUCT.

The EEOC guidelines hold that an employer *is* liable for *any* conduct constituting sexual harassment by its supervisors, whether those actions cause a job detriment or create a hostile work environment. However, some federal courts have taken divergent views of an employer's strict liability for acts of supervisors in sexual harassment "hostile environment" cases.

Let's look at a few of these court cases and examine the thinking of the judges in reaching their decisions:

In *Henson v. City of Dundee,* a three-judge panel of a federal appeals court in Atlanta, Georgia (11th Circuit), ruled that in order for an employer to be found liable for a hostile work environment created by the sexual harassment of one of its supervisors, it must have had actual or constructive knowledge of the harassment *and* have failed to take immediate, corrective action. The court based its conclusion on a belief that when a supervisor acts to create a hostile or offensive work environment, "he generally does it for his reasons and by his own means." On the other hand, in a job detriment case, the supervisor "uses the means furnished to him by the employer to accomplish the prohibited purpose."

One judge dissented from this position in writing his own opinion to state that he believed that any supervisor, by virtue of his position, does have the ability to create an offensive environment "when compared to the janitor, for example." He added: "When a supervisor creates such an environment, women employees are not apt to complain for fear of retaliation." [29 FEP Cases 787 (llth Cir. 1982)]

In two other cases, *Vinson v. Taylor* and *Jeppsen v. Wunnicke,* the courts (one an appellate court and the other a district court) take an opposite view. These courts followed the EEOC guidelines on sexual harassment and do not modify the strict liability rule just because the sexual harassment created a hostile environment rather than a job detriment. Making these kinds of distinctions in sexual harassment cases, the judge in *Jeppsen* wrote, is "extremely slippery" because there is a "seemingly endless variety of sexual harassment cases that blend into another when comparisons are made." He rejected the notion that the employer should have notice in one case but not the other in order to be held liable.

When court decisions differ in their conclusions like this, it is said, in legal jargon, that there is a "split of authority." Here, two federal courts of appeal (one, *Henson,* in Atlanta, Georgia, and the other *Vinson,* in the District of Columbia) have both looked at the same legal question and have come up with a different result. A split of authority in the Circuit Courts is not unusual. It means that, at the worst, there is a different opinion in different parts of the country. (Circuits for the federal appellate courts are set up regionally. For example, the Second Circuit Court of Appeals includes the states of New York and Connecticut.)

But the U.S. Supreme Court, the highest federal appellate court in the country, recently decided that the federal court of appeals in *Vinson* was a bit hasty in imposing strict liability upon the employer [*Meritor Savings Bank, FSB. v. Mechelle Vinson,* 54 U.S. Law Week 4703 (June 19, 1986)]. While declining to issue a definitive rule on employer liability, the Court did say that the federal court of appeals erred in concluding that employers are *always* automatically liable for sexual harassment of their supervisors who create a "hostile environment." The Supreme Court sent the case back to the court of appeals, instructing them to look at the "totality of the circumstances" in the case and decide if the employer bank was liable here, absent notice of the sexual harassment.

At best, as the situation now stands, the Supreme Court may one day hear another "hostile environment" sexual harassment case and finally decide to what extent an employer is legally liable for supervisors who sexually harass.

In the meantime, this legal "splitting of hairs" about an employer's sexual harassment liability leaves the rule unsettled and not very instructive to employers who are trying to deal with sexual harassment in their workplace. But these cases do indicate one thing clearly—the strict liability rule may be eroded in time. This is *not* to say that employers someday will no longer be liable for the actions of employees who sexually harass. It does mean that the courts may be willing to look carefully when an employer has notice of a supervisor's conduct and *does* take immediate corrective action. Remember, the reason for the strict liability rule is to give employers a legal incentive to eradicate sexual harassment from their workplaces. If the rule begins to accomplish that purpose, then the courts may apply it less onerously. One case that already portends that possibility is *Ferguson v. DuPont,* decided in 1983, one year after the *Henson* decision. Here a Delaware federal district court found that an employer was not liable in a Title VII lawsuit filed by a secretarial employee who alleged that her supervisor had created a hostile work environment with his abusive and sexist conduct. When she complained to the company, it launched an investigation and concluded that the supervisor had made statements that were perceived as sexual harassment by the secretary. As a reprimand, both the division manager of the department and the department manager made it clear to the harasser that his conduct would not be tolerated. The plaintiff conceded at trial that following this company action, the offensive behavior ceased. The court ruled that the employer was not liable, since, upon notice, it immediately took "strict and prompt remedial measures and strictly enforced well-known company policies." [31 FEP Cases 795, 814 (D. Delaware, 1983)]

Thus, the *Ferguson* decision is an example of how the rule of strict liability may be modified in the future if the courts can find immediate corrective action by an employer.

RULE #3: AN EMPLOYER IS LEGALLY LIABLE FOR THE SEXUAL HARASSMENT OF ITS EMPLOYEES BY CO-WORKERS *ONLY* IF IT HAD ACTUAL OR CONSTRUCTIVE KNOWLEDGE *AND* DID NOT TAKE IMMEDIATE CORRECTIVE ACTION.

Up to now, we have discussed the employer's responsibility for the actions of its supervisors. An employer can also be liable for the conduct of co-workers who sexually harass but here, EEOC guidelines on sexual harassment set a lower standard of liability than in the case of supervisor harassment. This means that an employer can raise a defense that it did not have notice of the sexual harassment. However, if the employer does have knowledge, it still must take immediate corrective action in order to escape legal liability.

In the majority of the court cases involving co-workers, sexual harassment takes the form of creating a hostile work environment since a co-worker does not have authority over a fellow employee so that he or she can condition a job decision upon acquiescence to sexual harassment. (In one case, *Robson v. Eva's Supermarket,* an Ohio federal district court found that a co-worker who was sexually harassing the plaintiff did have some supervisory authority so that the employer could be held to the standard of liability for a supervisor. [30 FEP Cases 1213, 1217 (N.D. Ohio, 1982)])

Thus, the legal doctrine of *respondeat superior* embodied in Title VII does not apply in co-worker cases. Instead, the EEOC and the courts look to an employer's legal responsibility to maintain a work environment free of discriminatory harassment for its employees.

Let's look at some cases under this rule:

—A federal employee alleged she was sexually harassed by a fellow employee and then later by two of her direct supervisors. She complained both formally and informally over a number of years but the employer took no corrective action. The federal appellate court in Richmond, Virginia (Fourth Circuit), court found that the sexual harassment of women in this employer's workplace was "standard operating procedure" which injected the "most demeaning sexual stereotypes...always represent(ing) an intentional assault on an individual's innermost privacy." Most important, the court ruled that the employer "permitted" this environment to continue even after the plaintiff's complaints because the employer did not take what it called the "ritual" of harassment of women seriously. [*Katz v. Dole,* 31 FEP Cases 1521 (4th Cir. 1983)]

—A female "personal banker" alleged she was sexually harassed by a male "personal banker" when they attended a two-day conference together. She claimed that on the way to and during the conference, he talked about sexual activity and touched her in an offensive way. A male assistant bank manager, who was also present, did not intervene. Upon returning from the conference, she complained to the vice president who conducted an investigation. Within four days of the complaint, the two men were disciplined—the assistant bank manager for his failure to intervene on behalf of the woman and the co-worker for his "grossly inappropriate" conduct. The co-worker was placed on a 90-day probation and given a warning that if such misconduct occurred again, he would be discharged. The federal appellate court in St. Louis, Missouri (8th Circuit), found that even though a full investigation into the matter did not lead to a discharge of the male employees, the court ruled that the employer did take remedial action that was "reasonably calculated to end the harassment." Thus the employer was not liable for the sexual harassment. [*Barrett v. Omaha National Bank,* 35 FEP Cases 594, 595 (8th Cir. 1984)]

RULE #4: AN EMPLOYER IS LIABLE FOR THE ACTS OF *NONEMPLOYEES* WHO SEXUALLY HARASS EMPLOYEES IN ITS WORKPLACE *ONLY IF* THE EMPLOYER HAS ACTUAL OR CONSTRUCTIVE KNOWLEDGE OF THE HARASSMENT AND HAS FAILED TO TAKE IMMEDIATE AND APPROPRIATE CORRECTIVE ACTION.

In addition to co-workers, an employer can also be liable under the EEOC guidelines on sexual harassment for the conduct of nonemployees who sexually harass its workers. This nonemployee can be a customer, business visitor, client or even the public. A court decision in a New York federal district court is most illustrative of this rule.

—A female lobby attendant in a Manhattan office building alleged that she was subjected to sexual propositions and lewd comments and gestures by people entering the lobby of the building. This was because she was required to wear a revealing costume on the job which was designed so that it exposed the sides of her upper body with no blouse or shirt underneath. She complained to management about the costume but was ultimately given the choice of wearing the costume or losing her job. The court found that since the wearing of the uniform was a requirement of the job, the sexual harassment that ensued was the responsibility of the employer which had the power to change the costume and did not. [*EEOC v. Sage Realty Corp.*, 24 FEP Cases 1521 (S.D.N.Y. 1981)]

RULE #5: AN EMPLOYER MAY BE LEGALLY LIABLE FOR UNLAWFUL SEX DISCRIMINATION IF IT GIVES EMPLOYMENT OPPORTUNITIES OR BENEFITS TO EMPLOYEES WHO SUBMITTED TO SEXUAL ADVANCES BUT NOT TO OTHER EMPLOYEES, WHO WERE QUALIFIED BUT DENIED, THOSE EMPLOYMENT OPPORTUNITIES OR BENEFITS.

A final rule under the EEOC guidelines on sexual harassment has to do with the employee who may lose out on a job benefit because someone else is giving in to sexual demands. This situation is commonly known as "sleeping one's way to the top" and is destructive for all individuals involved.

First, the supervisor who is accepting sexual favors is engaging in illegal conduct. The employee, who is now involved with the supervisor, may find she suffers a job detriment in the future when she wishes to break off the relationship. (At least one court has recognized that an employee in a once-consensual sexual relationship can later sue for sexual harassment. We'll discuss this case in the last chapter.) Finally, the employee who has not been offered the chance to exchange sexual favors for job advancement (and who may not wish to do so), is clearly affected by this situation.

Let's look at two cases that have been litigated on this issue.

—A female nurse alleges that she lost out on a promotion to a less-qualified nurse because that nurse was involved in a sexual relationship with the doctor who controlled the promotion. The federal district court in the District of Columbia ruled that although the plaintiff was not a direct target of the sexual advances, she would not have been subjected to this behavior but for her gender. Thus, this constitutes sex discrimination in violation of Title VII. However, here the court found no direct evidence of a sexual relationship between the doctor and the nurse and stated that cases like this "must not rest on rumor, knowing winks and prurient overtones." [*King v. Palmer,* 35 FEP Cases 1302 (D. D.C. 1984)]

—A female hospital administrator alleged that she was denied job advancement because the chief administrator conditioned the promotion she sought upon his receiving sexual favors from the individual promoted. Following the trial, the Delaware federal district court concluded that this administrator had engaged in such conduct because it believed that this man, a self-described "womanizer," demonstrated a total inability to separate his work life from "personal matters." There was direct evidence that he was involved in a sexual relationship with the woman who was promoted over the plaintiff and that her qualifications were not equal to the plaintiff's. The court held the employer liable for the actions of the supervisor, noting that his superiors not only failed to take prompt and remedial action when notified of the sexual harassment, but also they actually gave him a promotion! [*Toscano v. Nimmo*, 32 FEP Cases 1401 (D. Delaware 1983)]

All of these rules about the liability of the employer for conduct that constitutes sexual harassment either by supervisors, co-workers or nonemployees, have much to do with the kind of response an employer makes to the presence of sexual harassment in its workplace. Even with a strict liability rule for supervisors, we have seen some leeway if the employer takes prompt, appropriate remedial action.

But what is striking about the sexual harassment cases that have gone to court is that in most the employer is held liable because of failure to act—even with actual knowledge that the sexual harassment is going on! A survey of court decisions across the country since 1976 finds many employers lost because they did not act upon a complaint, or investigated it poorly.

Here are a few of the more striking examples: (The first was previously discussed, but look at it again—this time with the employer's responses to the victim's complaints included.)

—Initially, a female worker, who was one of only two women in the employer's warehouse, complained to her supervisor that one male co-worker asked her on several different occasions if she was wearing a bra. The supervisor responded by telling the individual to "knock it off" but did not formally reprimand him. The harassment only increased from there and for the next three years, other co-workers joined in. One co-worker exposed his buttocks to the plaintiff 10-20 times with several witnesses to these incidents. When she complained to the plant manager, the individual was called into the front office, asked to apologize to the individual but refused. No disciplinary action was taken. Others also exposed their buttocks, made crude sexual remarks and called the plaintiff by offensive and abusive derogatory names for women. At trial, the two plant managers testified that the plaintiff complained about the situation to each of them, "more than several" times. Management's response was to hold occasional general meetings in which the company rules about abusive language were reviewed. No other disciplinary action was taken against any of the individual co-workers. Some male co-workers began posting drawings, many depicting naked women with exaggerated sexual features and some with the plaintiff's initials on them. When she complained about these drawings to the plant managers, a warehouse meeting was called to review the company's policy against postings. The drawings stopped for a while and then reappeared. When the plaintiff finally filed a complaint with the federal Equal Employment Opportunity Commission (EEOC), the company immediately launched an investigation, determined that sexual harassment had occurred and disciplined several individuals, including the discharge of one co-worker. But the Wisconsin federal district court found these company actions too little, too late. It determined that despite the general warehouse meetings, the harassment went on for more than three years and the company should have recognized that the meetings were not being effective. "Because the defendant and its officers were aware of the harassment but failed to adopt effective corrective measures," the court wrote, "they are liable for co-workers' acts." [*Zabkowicz v. West Bend Co.*, 35 FEP Cases 611 (D. Wisc. 1974)]

—Over a two-year period, a female secretary who was subjected to the sexual advances of her boss discussed the sexual harassment with several managers including a female vice president. When she was ultimately discharged for refusing to accede to his sexual demands, she complained to an executive vice president who was the immediate supervisor of the harasser. This vice president did not immediately act but subsequently did call the supervisor to ask about the plaintiff's allegations. When the accused denied that he had sexually harassed the plaintiff, the vice president dropped the matter. The Colorado federal district court ruled that the employer knew about the harassment early on and failed to investigate fully. In particular, the court noted that the executive vice president whom the plaintiff complained to following her termination did "nothing more than call the 'accused' for verification or denial." The employer was held liable for the sexual harassment. [*Heelan v. Johns-Manville Corp.*, 451 F. Supp 1382, 1389 (D. Colo. 1978)]

—A female employee of the Federal Aviation Administration, the only woman on a crew of air traffic controllers, was continually and seriously sexually harassed by co-workers and supervisors. The federal appellate court in Richmond, Virginia (Fourth Circuit), found that it developed into a "pattern of personally directed sexual insult and innuendo." Despite knowledge of the harassment, her employer's supervisory personnel did "nothing effectual to stop it and, indeed, took part in it," the court wrote. Although the FAA had a policy against sexual harassment, the court found that the agency knew it was ineffective and did nothing about it. The employer was held liable for the sexual harassment. [*Katz v. Dole,* 31 FEP Cases 1521, 1525 (4th Cir. 1983)]

What these cases show is that an employer can double or triple its exposure to liability when its managers become "accomplices" to the original acts of sexual harassment. By failing to investigate complaints properly, or worse yet, by totally refusing to take them seriously, management only exacerbates the problem instead of guiding it to a solution. Court decisions that clear employers of liability, on the other hand, cast management as *responsive* to complaints, *sensitive* to the plight of the victims and *active* in ridding the workplace of illegal sexual harassment.

Positive actions like these not only limit liability, but they also tend to stop sexual harassment at an early point in time.

Recall the personal banker case. The woman alleged only one act of sexual harassment. She reported it, and within four days there was a company action and the sexual harassment stopped. And also recall the case of the secretary, who after her complaint of sexual harassment by her supervisor was addressed by management, admitted that the sexual harassment ceased.

You can stop sexual harassment early because that is the point in time when the situation is most ripe for a solution, says Dr. Mary P. Rowe, Special Assistant to the President of the Masssachusetts Institute of Technology (MIT). Dr. Rowe, who has worked since 1974 as a mediator in hundreds of cases of harassment at MIT and in other corporations and institutions, wrote in a 1981 *Harvard Business Review* article:

"It is rare in my experience for a complainant to ask for any kind of retribution (against the harasser); nearly always this person simply wants it to stop."

In addition, she finds that the harasser, at this early stage, may be most able to see the situation in the same way as the victim—as a problem. Intervention of a third party (particularly someone outside the organization) merely polarizes each party's views and makes a simple solution impossible.

Thus, while legal responsibility for sexual harassment in the workplace falls squarely on the employer, a prudent employer that takes immediate corrective action upon a complaint of sexual harassment will profit by such a positive response. Legal liability for the sexual harassment can be avoided and, best of all, the harassment could easily be stopped early.

Chapter 3

What You Can Do about Sexual Harassment

Management can do much to combat sexual harassment in the workplace. That's the opinion of victims and supervisors in the 1981 study of the federal workplace by the U. S. Merit Systems Protection Board (MSPB). Most participants endorsed management actions to impose tougher sanctions against harassers and stricter enforcement of company policies prohibiting sexual harassment. In addition, the following management actions were overwhelmingly supported by both men and women:

1. Conduct swift and thorough investigations of complaints of sexual harassment.
2. Enforce penalties against managers who knowingly allow this behavior to continue or who sexually harass others.
3. Publicize the availability of in-house formal complaint channels.
4. Establish and publicize policies which prohibit sexual harassment.
5. Provide training for managers and EEO officers on their responsibilities for decreasing sexual harassment.

Your campaign to combat sexual harassment should include all of the above actions. The key to a successful campaign is to get your top management team to support it and the idea that sexual harassment can happen in your workplace.

What can you do to convince them? First, you can rely on surveys already completed on sexual harassment in the workplace. For example, the MSPB study on sexual harassment in the federal workplace was the first scientifically controlled survey of its kind. This in-depth study helped establish certain "facts" about sexual harassment, including its rate of incidence, the characteristics of the harasser and the harassed, and the perceptions of employees about sexual behavior in the workplace. A study of sexual harassment by *Harvard Business Review/Redbook* magazines is an especially valuable tool for letting your top management know how other executives in the country view sexual harassment in the workplace. The 2,000 male and female executives in the study shared their perceptions of the problem and revealed how they would personally confront it in their companies.

You can look to these surveys for facts to persuade top management that sexual harassment is occurring in your workplace and to support a campaign against it. Or you can conduct your own informal survey of sexual harassment. A sample employee survey is included in the booklet, *Sexual Harassment on the Job: A Guide for Employers,* published by the Massachusetts Advisory Committee to the U. S. Commission on Civil Rights. Find out how your employees feel about sexual harassment and management's response to it. Chances are your findings will mirror the studies mentioned above.

Here are some arguments you may get from your top management team about sexual harassment in your workplace.

1. **"It's happening somewhere else, but not here."**

    YOUR RESPONSE: As studies have shown, sexual harassment can occur in any workplace including the public sector, private industry, educational institutions or medical facilities. Wherever there is the potential for using conduct of a sexual nature to abuse power, sexual harassment will be present. Because of the grudging tolerance of sexual demands and abuse in the workplace for so many years, no workplace can claim that it has yet eradicated sexual harassment.

2. **"We are all such nice people, it can't be happening here."**

    YOUR RESPONSE: Sexual harassment has very little to do with being "nice." It is an abuse of power that may not be seen in public because it is much more effective as a one-on-one confrontation between the harasser and the harassed. It's happening in workplaces where there are some "nice" people who are also sexual harassers. It can happen here.

3. **"No one is complaining about it, so it's not happening here."**

    YOUR RESPONSE: Unless employees who are experiencing sexual harassment feel they will not be retaliated against for complaining, they will not come forward. Also, research shows that many complainers feel that their complaint will not be taken seriously so they do not bother to complain.

Finally, let your managers know that sexual harassment costs money! Look back at the figures from the MSPB study listed earlier in this book. See if you can estimate the cost of sexual harassment in your own company from unnecessary job turnover, increased use of health benefits, loss of productivity and a higher rate of absenteeism.

Why is it so important to involve top management? Because if attitudes about sexual harassment change at the top, they will trickle down. Employees take policies and procedures that have top management's backing seriously. You need top management to say sexual harassment is no joking matter, then the jokes and the abusive conduct will end.

Develop Your Policy

Once you have sold top management, your work to combat sexual harassment begins. You should start with a company policy that is a short, succinct statement that sexual harassment will not be tolerated. It should come from top management and be promulgated throughout your workplace including new-employee orientation programs.

Here's a checklist for you in writing a company policy against sexual harassment.

ITEMS TO INCLUDE IN A POLICY AGAINST SEXUAL HARASSMENT

___ State a purpose. It can be something like "to ensure a workplace free of sexual harassment" or "to treat employees in a fair and humane way without the presence of sexual harassment" or "to eradicate sexual harassment in our workplace."

___ Include a definition of sexual harassment. You can use a behavioral model or legal definition or both. Use examples of the different types of sexual harassment so employees will be clear about each.

___ Encourage employees to complain about sexual harassment.

___ Let them know that there will be disciplinary actions taken against any offenders. List some or all of the possible sanctions.

___ Tell them that sexual harassment is a serious problem taken seriously by management.

___ Emphasize that combating sexual harassment promotes good employee relations rather than "we can get sued."

This policy is the underpinning of all you do next. It sets forth your company's goal and commitment to deal seriously with sexual harassment.

Set Up Your Complaint Procedure

It is important to point out that several federal courts have said that even if an employer had a stated policy against sexual harassment, it can still be held legally liable because it failed to take immediate corrective action. This means that your next step is to set up an internal complaint procedure so that you can respond to individual cases of sexual harassment. You need a procedure tailored to your workplace. You can look at another company's procedure as a model but since no two companies are exactly alike, that procedure may not readily fit your workplace structures. Look to see if your existing internal complaint system will accommodate sexual harassment complaints. That way, employees will not be confused by too many complaint procedures.

On the other hand, a special procedure for sexual harassment can draw more attention to the problem. You can have specially trained company personnel handling these cases who may also act as counselors to support employees going through the process.

A recent U.S. Supreme Court decision in *Meritor Savings Bank, FSB. v. Mechelle Vinson* is instructive as to what kind of procedure to put in place. In that case, Vinson alleged her supervisor, a bank vice president, created a "hostile environment" by subjecting her to repeated unwelcomed sexual demands and attentions. Because she was afraid of him and the power he had over her as an employee, she consented to some of his demands but never reported any of his actions to his supervisors nor did she use the bank's complaint procedure. Vinson endured his behavior until she was fired for excessive use of sick days.

The Court rejected the bank's argument that it should not be liable for the sexual harassment because Vinson did not use the bank's internal grievance procedure before filing the federal lawsuit. The mere existence of such a procedure did not insulate the employer here from liability because the bank's general nondiscrimination policy did not address sexual harassment in particular. The Court wrote: "Thus, (it) did not alert employees to their employer's interest in correcting that form of discrimination." (54 U.S. Law Week at 4708.) Also, the court noted that the bank's grievance procedure required an employee to complain first to her supervisor, in this case, the man who was in fact harassing Vinson.

Whether sexual harassment complaints are incorporated into an existing complaint procedure or a specific one is set up only for these cases, the procedure should include both a formal and an informal complaint mechanism. As will be discussed later, sometimes an informal process resolves complaints faster. Because an employee who is experiencing sexual harassment can remain anonymous in an informal process, he or she may feel more comfortable discussing the problem with the company.

The formal part of the process allows each party to present evidence and call witnesses in an objective forum. You should decide who or what body will hear these complaints and make recommendations for action. Some companies have designated an affirmative action officer while others have developed special boards or committees with representatives of both management and employees participating.

Encourage Complaints

Your complaint procedure, however it may look, should be designed to *encourage* complaints of sexual harassment. Why? Because research shows and several court decisions have recognized that it is difficult for employers to come forward with complaints of sexual harassment. In *Jeppsen v. Wunnicke,* 37 FEP Cases 994 (D. Alaska, 1985), an Alaska federal district court noted that the employee who stays the longest on the job and puts up with the most offensive sexual harassment will probably be the employee who is most financially dependent on her job. She is reticent to complain because she fears losing her job or not getting an adequate response to her complaint from her employer. (In *Bundy v. Jackson,* a federal worker complained to her supervisor about the unwelcome sexual advances of a fellow employee and he casually dismissed the complaint by telling her, "Any man in his right mind would want to rape you.")

You can help an employee experiencing sexual harassment who is not able to come forward by providing in your procedure that *any* employee can make a complaint, at least an informal one. Think about it:—everyone in a workplace suffers when there is sexual harassment, even if they are not the direct target of it.

Encouraging complaints of sexual harassment means you can retain valuable employees. Here is an example from a recent court case. A bank teller was sexually harassed for more than four years by her supervisor. She finally began to take extended sick leave because she could not face the sexual harassment daily but she was eventully fired for abuse of sick time. But did anyone—a supervisor, manager or even a co-worker—ask this employee why she was taking so much sick leave? Was something wrong at work? Something management could do? Moreover, this employee could have been encouraged to file a complaint about the sexual harassment or another employee could have done so, so that the problem was brought to management's attention for corrective action. Instead, an employer lost a seasoned, trained employee because of sexual harassment. [*Vinson v. Taylor,* 36 FEP Cases 1423 (D.C. Cir. 1985)]

Another reason to encourage complaints lies in your legal responsibility for sexual harassment. Recall that under the strict liability rule, an employer is liable:

1. for sexual harassment by supervisors *even* if it had no knowledge, and

2. for sexual harassment by co-workers or nonemployees *unless* it had knowledge *and* took corrective action.

A sexual harassment complaint procedure is extremely valuable when an employee alleges sexual harassment by a co-worker or nonemployee because it can provide an immediate response to the complaint and a mechanism for corrective action. Even if the complaint involves a supervisor, a situation in which an employer cannot raise a legal defense that it had no knowledge of the sexual harassment, having a complaint is better than not having one. The complaint is an opportunity to end the harassment and avoid a lawsuit.

Don't be afraid that setting up a procedure will result in too many complaints. That means that you are reaching your audience and providing an internal mechanism that is well-perceived by your employees. If you handle these complaints fairly and efficiently, you will build trust in the sytem and the number of complaints will decrease.

Who Should Handle Complaints?

Whoever you pick to handle these complaints must be someone who is viewed as credible, objective, sensitive and trustworthy. In order to achieve this in an internal complaint program, some companies have created an ombudsperson to deal with complaints of harassment. Dr. Mary Rowe of the Massachusetts Institute of Technology is an ombudsperson, who, as Special Assistant to the President, works with students, faculty and employees to resolve problems like sexual harassment.

How to Handle Complaints

In many cases, Dr. Mary Rowe utilizes mediation and other forms of conflict resolution. For example, from her work with sexual harassment complaints, she has developed an effective informal process for some cases in which the victim or the alleged harasser have little understanding of the other's point of view. Before an intervening third party (e.g. another supervisor, a manager or even an ombudsperson) polarizes each party's view of the situation, Dr. Rowe finds that a discussion between these two parties can help.

To facilitate such a discussion, she suggests a letter written by the offended employee to the offender with three specific parts. The first part precisely relates the *facts* of what happened and when. For example, "On Friday night, you rubbed my back and touched my breast." The second part tells the offender how his conduct made her *feel*. For example, "I was embarrassed by your behavior," " I wanted to leave my job," or "I was scared." It should also include how his behavior affected her life. For example, "I couldn't sleep," "I was depressed.")

Finally, the letter states what she would like to have happen. For example, "I would like you to stop" or "I would like to have my last evaluation redone so it can be fair." Dr Rowe suggests that the letter be hand-delivered to the individual so that it can remain confidential. Following delivery of the letter, she reports that sometimes there is an apology or a denial or the beginning of a discussion or silence. But nearly always, the sexual harassment stops.

Utilizing the skills and resources of an ombudsperson like Dr. Rowe is one way to provide an effective informal channel in your company. You can designate others for the task too; but in either case you should make every effort to resolve complaints of sexual harassment informally. By focusing on the allegations in the informal process as Dr. Rowe outlines, you can clarify:

1. how the conduct is offensive to the employee in a factual way,

2. how the behavior makes her feel and how it affects her life, and

3. what actions by the harasser or the company would resolve the problem satisfactorily.

Once you have established the needs and feelings of the complainant, then a confrontation with the alleged harasser can be nonthreatening and effective. Yet not all complaints can be resolved informally, particularly by a letter to the offending employee. Nor does this action exonerate an employer from doing more. But informal actions can reduce the possibilities that the complainant will suffer retaliation, which usually results from the bad feelings created when a third party intervenes. Nonetheless, retaliation against an employee who complains should be prohibited in your procedure as a separate violation of the company policy against sexual harassment. Retaliation for complaining about an employment condition that violates federal antidiscrimination laws (such as sexual harassment) is prohibited by Title VII.

Here is a checklist for you to use in setting up an internal complaint procedure for sexual harassment.

CHECKLIST FOR SETTING UP AN INTERNAL COMPLAINT PROCEDURE

___ DEFINITION OF SEXUAL HARASSMENT—Include a definition of sexual harassment with clear examples. Many companies use the definition in the EEOC guidelines, but you can have a behavioral model too. This should be consistent with any definition in company policy against sexual harassment.

___ FORMAL AND INFORMAL MECHANISM—Include both:

INFORMAL—Give employees a place to go to talk where they can remain anonymous and no written records will be kept. The employee can decide to confront the alleged harasser in the informal process, either by letter, as Dr. Mary Rowe suggests, or in person, with or without the presence of another company employee.

FORMAL—If there is no resolution in the informal process, or the charges of sexual harassment are serious, provide a formal complaint mechanism. Then, an employee name must be included in the complaint and a written record is kept. The process includes an investigation, fact-finding hearing and an appeal.

___ CONFIDENTIALITY—Victims of sexual harassment should decide when their names will be disclosed—not management. In the informal process, it should not be necessary to reveal the complainant's name. You can require it later if a formal complaint is made.

___ RECORDKEEPING FUNCTION—You can choose to keep a written record of all complaints filed, even those in the informal process. But since an informal complaint (particularly an anonymous one) is only an allegation, keeping a written record of it could be unfair to the alleged harasser, who has no knowledge of the complaint and has had no chance to have his/her side of the story included in the file.

___ INVESTIGATION AND HEARING PROCESS—A hearing can be held if an investigation does not resolve the complaint. (See below for a checklist on investigations.) Decide who or what body will hear the complaint and how formal the hearing will be. A decision should indicate what facts the decision-maker relied on and what action is recommended.

___ APPEAL—Allow either party to appeal a hearing decision, but that does not mean that the case will be given another hearing. In an appeal, the evidence gathered in the hearing and investigation is reviewed to see if the decision reached was reasonable. This review can be done by one individual or a series of individuals in top management all the way to the company president if you wish.

___ TIME LINES—Set limitations on how long each step can take. (e.g. "The findings and recommendations of the hearing officer shall be issued within 10 days of the hearing.") Important points in the process that need time lines are completing the investigation, scheduling a date for the hearing, reaching a decision, filing an appeal, and deciding the appeal. Also, set a "statute of limitations," the time period within which an employee must complain about the sexual harassment. It should be long enough so that, for example, the employee could transfer from the particular job where she is being harassed before making the complaint but not so long that everyone will have forgotten what had happened.

___ OPTIONS—Provide employees experiencing harassment with several places to complain so they do not have to complain to the harasser or someone with whom they do not feel comfortable. Employees should also be informed of their legal rights to complain outside the company.

___ SANCTIONS AND DISCIPLINE FOR HARASSERS—Include a list of possible sanctions and progressive discipline for any employee found to have sexually harassed another employee.

___ PUBLICITY—Inform employees of the procedure through a vigorous in-house publicity campaign including posting throughout the workplace and informing all new employees through the orientation program.

___ REVIEW OF THE PROCEDURE—Look at your procedure annually for ways to improve it. Get feedback from employees and managers. Also, provide them with an annual report on the effectiveness of the procedure including number of complaints, final outcomes and publicity efforts.

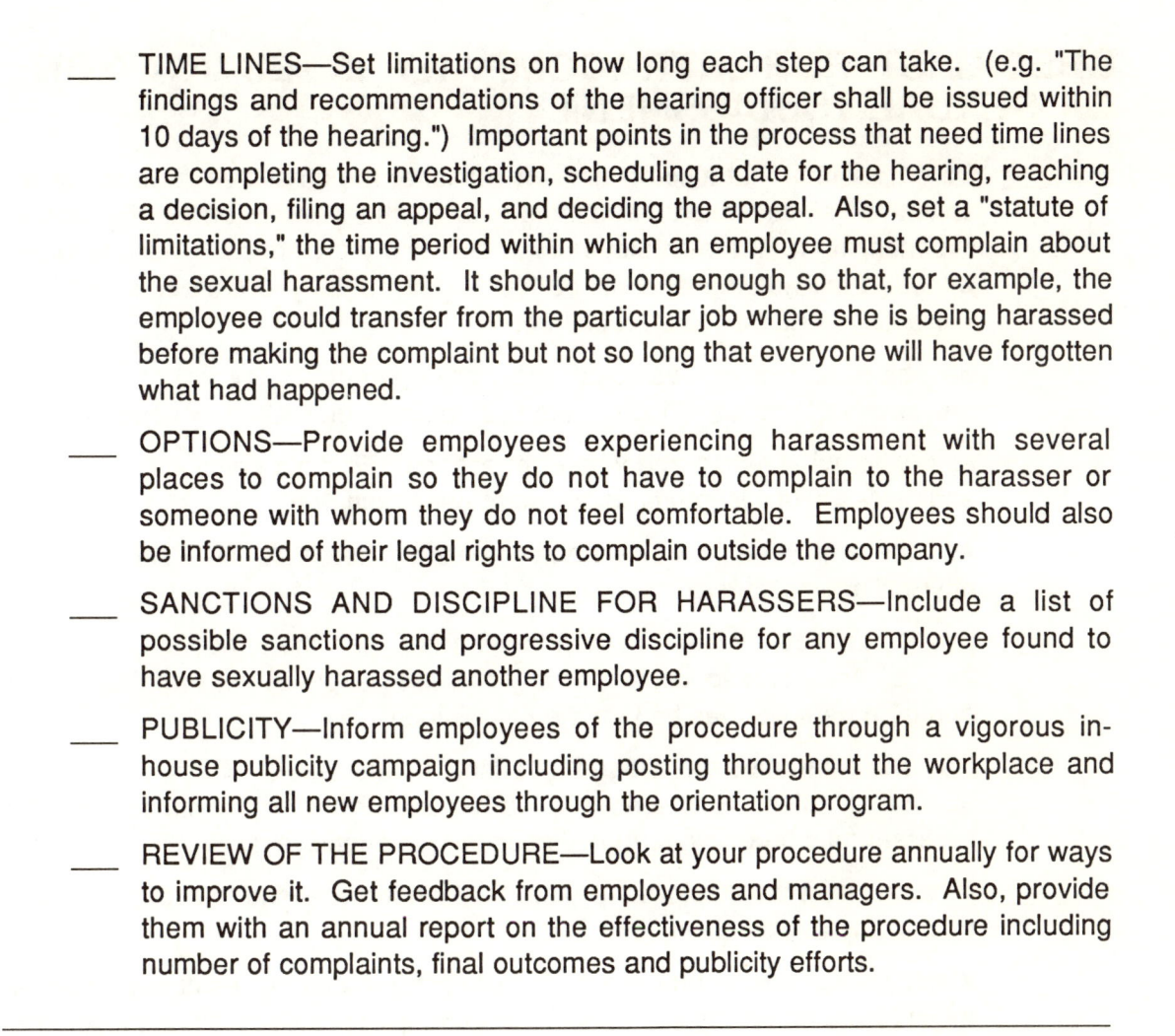

Investigations are an integral part of the internal complaint procedure because they can be the most impartial response to a complaint if they are done properly. It is your company's chance to show that it can be thorough, non-judgmental and fair in handling complaints of sexual harassment.

Remember, as discussed previously, companies who fail to act upon complaints of sexual harassment are vulnerable to litigation and fail to build employee trust in the internal complaint system.

CHECKLIST FOR INTRACOMPANY INVESTIGATION OF SEXUAL HARASSMENT

___ Do not assume that a complaint is frivolous or the employee is being "overly sensitive" since sexual harassment is in the perception of the person experiencing it. If the employee feels that you are dismissing her complaint without a fair hearing, she will be less willing to tell you the details and you will lessen her trust in the procedure.

___ Be objective, fair, professional and nonjudgmental. Try not to have any preconceived notions. Find out the facts before you make any conclusions.

___ Ask "who, what, when and where" questions. Find out specific dates, times and places. How long has harassment been going on?

___ Ask the employee how this behavior makes her feel. Has she had any physical effects from it?

___ Has the employee talked to others about this? Has she turned to co-workers, friends, family or a spouse? Can any of these people confirm what effect this offensive behavior has had on the complainant's life?

___ Has she confronted the alleged harasser? What result? If not, counsel her about that option. How serious is the harassment? If it is a subtle form, the harasser may be unaware that his behavior is offensive.

___ If you suspect the employee is lying, think about what she has to gain or lose by bringing a false claim.

___ Identify witnesses for both sides. Talk to present employees about what they might have seen or heard. Talk to former employees since an employee may have left because of sexual harassment by the same individual. Several court decisions have stressed that the testimony of witnesses, who may have been harassed themselves, is relevant in a sexual harassment case, notably one in which there are allegations of a "hostile environment."

___ Establish who the alleged harasser is. Ask him about each incident of sexual harassment. Consider age, years and performance with the company, and any previous complaints of sexual harassment. Determine his attitude towards the seriousness of sexual harassment on the job. And remember, several courts have found that dropping an investigation because the individual denies allegations of sexual harassment is not acceptable.

___ Make sure the employee who has made the complaint has people supporting her. Explain the process to her as you go along. (e.g. "The next step is a fact-finding hearing and then an appeal if the determination is against you.")

When You Find Harassment

With a thorough and fair investigation of complaints of sexual harassment followed by a fact-finding hearing, if necessary, your internal complaint procedure will be finding that, in some cases, sexual harassment did occur. If so, discipline for the harasser should be appropriate, realistic and consistent.

• **Sanctions should fit the offense.** It may not be appropriate to fire an employee who has been found to have harassed *one* employee on *one* occasion with obscene language or gestures. Instead, you may want this employee to know that his or her behavior is not acceptable and if it continues, there will be a more serious reprimand. You may also want to note the circumstances and outcome of the complaint in that employee's personnel file. On the other hand, discharging an employee who is found to have assaulted or been very abusive, *even once,* may also be appropriate.

• **Do not contradict your company's usual progressive discipline system.** You should not discipline any more or less harshly just because it is a sexual harassment case.

• **Finally, treat harassers equally.** Treat every employee who is found to have sexually harassed another employee in the same way—whether the individual is top management or an hourly employee. Employees will have no faith in a system that does not discipline consistently. Sanctions should also be used not only against the harasser, but also against any member of management who has knowingly allowed sexual harassment to continue after complaints were made.

Conducting an Investigation

Several federal courts have upheld a company's right to discipline following a proper investigation of a sexual harassment complaint. However, the investigation should be thorough and immediate. In *French v. Mead Corp.*, the Ohio federal district court ruled that an employee properly discharged a foreman who was found to have sexually harassed at least four female subordinates. Prior to the discharge, the court found that the employer's labor relations manager had thoroughly investigated the matter and the operations manager had confronted the harasser and all other witnesses. [33 FEP Cases 635 (S.D.Ohio, 1983]

Likewise, a federal bankruptcy court in the state of Washington allowed the removal of a bankruptcy trustee who was found, after a hearing, to have sexually harassed female employees. The court noted there was a "strong Federal policy against women employees being forced to endure offensive and unwelcome sexual advances by their supervisor or employer." [*In the Matter of Chapter 13,* 33 FEP Cases 1871 (U.S. Bankruptcy Court, Washington 1982)]

However, an employee should not be removed before an adequate investigation. For example, in *Huff v. County of Butler,* no hearing was afforded a male supervisor who was fired after a female subordinate made several complaints of sexual harassment. He was given the option of being fired or resigning voluntarily and getting unemployment compensation. Although he denied the charges, he resigned because he did not want to lose the benefits. The Pennsylvania federal district court determined that, without an investigation or hearing on the complaints of sexual harassment, the supervisor was denied "liberty" without due process of law. His forced resignation "stigmatized" him and damaged his reputation and character in his community. The court concluded he should have had the opportunity to prove his allegations in court. [27 FEP Cases 63 (W. D. Penna. 1981)]

In addition, if you employ blue-collar workers, investigators of sexual harassment complaints should be alert to novel conditions in that setting that contribute to the sexual harassment of workers. As mentioned before, women are often victims of sexual harassment in nontraditional jobs—many of which are blue-collar occupations such as factory labor, construction or police work—because male co-workers usually outnumber them and can engage in inappropriate sexual behavior to discourage them in those jobs. Several federal courts have noted that these occupations are dangerous or involve machinery that entails the labor of several workers simultaneously. This means that employees must work in teams in close proximity to each other. In addition, some physical touching is necessary in order to communicate over the din of machinery in motion. These conditions provide some co-workers with an opportunity to act in offensive or abusive ways. For example, a male co-worker touches a female worker on the breast as a way to signal her to stop the machine. A touching was necessary but this was offensive and inappropriate. Or a woman is assigned to a work team which includes several male co-workers who harass her throughout the shift by referring to the machinery operation in sexual terms that are offensive to her.

The blue-collar workplace is also known for its rough language and crude horseplay. Sometimes female employees join in and do not seem to be offended by it. In some cases, the courts have found that these women were not subjected to sexual harassment. Other times, when the females complain about the offensive behavior, the courts have acknowledged that an employer must conduct a very active and on-going campaign to stop *all* such conduct.

An employer should make allowance for the above conditions when investigating the sexual harassment of blue-collar workers, but still recognize that sexual harassment is prevalent in such a setting. In *Zabkowicz v. West Bend Co.,* the Wisconsin federal district court did find that a female warehouse worker was "tormented" by her male co-workers over a three-year period and determined that the employer identified the offending employees in an immediate thorough investigation of the sexual harassment and disciplined them for their conduct.

Training Is the Final Step

The final step of your campaign against sexual harassment is a comprehensive training program that will involve every employee in your workplace. This program should provide information on what sexual harassment is and how your company is combating it. It should emphasize the company policy against sexual harassment and explain how the internal complaint procedure works. In addition, the training can be a time when all employees can talk, preferably in small groups, openly and frankly about the problem of sexual harassment and come up with recommendations for stopping it.

You can also train your employees to deal effectively with other employees who are annoying or harassing them. Dramatize sexual harassment cases and let employees respond as if they were in that situation. Have employees play some of the roles themselves so that they can practice confronting a harasser or making a complaint to management about sexual harassment. Use these methods with supervisors and top managers, too, to teach them how to handle complaints, recognize sexual harassment and confront harassers on the job.

Do not be afraid to "enlighten" your employees about sexual harassment. It can only get the message out and give employees new skills for handling sexual harassment immediately and effectively. Through this training, every employee will know that the company is taking action against sexual harassment. This action in specific cases of sexual harassment will be responsive and corrective to change the behavior of some employees who do not think they are doing anything offensive or who think that the company disapproves of it. For those who intentionally use their power in the workplace to sexually harass others, the company's action will tell them that such conduct will not be tolerated.

For a broader attack on sexual harassment, the company actions should be to effect an attitudinal change about sexual harassment in the workplace. This means having employees examine their attitudes about their relationships to each other and how they use or abuse power in a sexual way. Changes in attitude about sexual harassment have to be gradual because it will take time to break down the grudging tolerance of sexual harassment that presently exists. One way to begin is to make training on sexual harassment a part of your company's on-going equal employment opportunity program.

With such a responsive, corrective and active campaign against sexual harassment, the future holds the prospect that you can eradicate it in your workplace.

Chapter 4

What Lies Ahead?

Before viewing the future, let's review what we have learned about sexual harassment—one of the important equal employment opportunity issues of the decade.

—Sexual harassment has been documented as a serious problem in workplaces of every size and description.

—It constitutes a serious invasion of an employee's privacy and can affect his or her health and well-being. It is an identified cause of lower productivity on the job, increased job dissatisfaction and a higher absenteeism rate. It can cost an employer seasoned, trained employees, increase the use of job benefit programs and incur litigation expenses.

—Federal courts across the country have found sexual harassment to be illegal sex discrimination under Title VII of the Civil Rights Act of 1964. A *prima facie* case of sexual harassment includes proof that the sexual attentions were unwanted and job-related.

—An employer is responsible for the sexual harassment of its employees by supervisors, co-workers and nonemployees, depending on the knowledge it had of the sexual harassment and its efforts to take immediate corrective action.

—Employers can do much to combat sexual harassment by establishing a company policy against sexual harassment, setting up an internal complaint procedure and training all employees to be sensitive to the problem.

What Lies Ahead?

The U.S. Supreme Court's recent decision in *Meritor Savings Bank, FSB. v. Mechelle Vinson,* 54 U.S. Law Week 4703 (June 19,1986), affirmed that sexual harassment is sex discrimination under Title VII. But the high court left some questions in the case unsettled. An important one is what is the definitive rule under Title VII that holds an employer is liable for a supervisor's conduct when it creates a "hostile environment"?

Other legal questions about sexual harassment not posed in *Meritor Savings Bank,* may one day reach the U.S. Supreme Court also. These include what constitutes a *prima facie* case of sexual harassment under Title VII and to what extent are employers liable for co-workers, nonemployees and customers who sexually harass? Because the high court is the final arbiter of legal questions in our system, until a case is taken by the Court which addresses these issues again or for the first time, much of the Title VII law about sexual harassment is, in legal terms, "unsettled."

How Cases Are Litigated

Nonetheless, creative litigators who represent employees experiencing sexual harassment are not waiting for the final pronouncement on Title VII from the Supreme Court. They are suing employers for sexual harassment under other legal causes of action which include:

—breach of contract, claiming that the sexual misconduct of a third party (e.g. a supervisor) interfered with an employee's contractual rights including the right to a workplace free of sexual harassment,

—civil tort actions, e.g. "assault and battery" or "intentional infliction of emotional distress," which allow claims for punitive damages and a jury trial,

—claims under state employment discrimination laws, when they provide a private right of action in state court and, in some states, a jury trial,

—workers' compensation, alleging that stress and stress-related injuries are "on-the-job" injuries under state laws,

—unemployment compensation, when state law provides that an employee is not disqualified from receiving benefits if she left for "good cause" and sexual harassment has been found to be "good cause,"

—criminal sanctions against the harasser individually for behaviors that constitute criminal sexual assault under state laws, and,

—successful defense of libel and defamation suits brought against a victim for allegedly maligning the reputation of an individual by making false accusations of sexual harassment in the community.

These new emerging legal actions are important because relief under Title VII is limited to "compensatory damages." That is, the court will order that an employer pay the plaintiff only what he or she actually lost—usually back pay or job reinstatement, if discharge was at issue. In some other legal actions, however, the court can award punitive damages, which are beyond what the plaintiff actually lost and compensate for more ephemeral items as "pain and suffering," "humiliation" or "embarrassment." In addition, Title VII cases are only heard by a judge who renders a decision after a trial and sets damages if the plaintiff wins. Jury trials, on the other hand, are allowed in some of these other legal actions and jury damage awards are usually larger than those given by judges. For example, a Michigan state court jury awarded a woman $180,000 in damages in a sexual harassment suit against her employer. In Wisconsin, a federal district court vacated an award of $200,000 in damages (including $105,000 in punitive damages) set by a jury for a male victim of sexual harassment. [*Huebschen v. Dept. Health*, 32 FEP Cases 1521 (W. D. Wisconsin 1982)]

An Increase in Complaints

Besides more litigation, an increase in sexual harassment complaints by workers also appears to be on the horizon. Why? One answer is that the Women's Bureau of the U.S. Department of Labor projects more American women will be joining the labor force, particularly in male-dominated occupations and industries. Although men can be victims too, sexual harassment is still a problem faced, for the most part, by women workers. Thus, as more women enter and men hold most of the power in the workplace, there is the potential for these new workers to be victimized by abuses of power through sexual harassment. (Interestingly, the majority of executives in the joint *Harvard Business Review/Redbook* survey on sexual harassment did not expect that as women gain more power, they would abuse it in the same sexual ways as men.) Furthermore, because these women will be entering nontraditional fields, they will be more likely to be sexually harassed (unless management is conscientious) as a way to discourage them in those jobs.

Another answer can be found in the fact that sexual harassment is a very visible workplace issue today with articles about it being given prominent play in all the news media. As more and more employees learn that what is happening to them is not an isolated incident, they will more vociferously assert their rights to a workplace free of sexual harassment.

Along with this increase in the number of sexual harassment complaints will come more involving the subtler forms of sexual harassment—those alleging, for example, that unwanted sexual attentions created a hostile, intimidating and offensive work environment rather than caused a job detriment. The number of lawsuits being filed in this category has been increasing since *Bundy v. Jackson* established a cause of action for such allegations in 1981.

Job Detriment

In the "job detriment" arena of sexual harassment litigation, the federal courts may soon wrestle with a lawsuit in which an employer raises a defense that the alleged harasser made sexual advances to *both* male and female workers. Such a case would raise a unique legal issue because the legal theory that sexual harassment is sex discrimination under Title VII is premised on the notion that, but for her sex, a woman would not have been subjected to sexual harassment. This principle was established in the 1977 appeal of a 1974 lower court decision, *Barnes v. Train,* 13 FEP Cases 123 (D.D.C. 1974). The lower court ruled a female federal worker, who refused to have an "after-hours" affair with her boss, was indeed retaliated against for her refusal, but this was not because she was a woman. Instead, the retaliation came because she refused to engage in a personal affair with a supervisor. The appellate court for the District of Columbia found this reasoning "disingenuous in the extreme" and wrote: "To say that she was victimized in her employment simply because she declined the invitation is to ignore the asserted fact that she was invited only because she was a woman subordinate to the inviter." [*Barnes v. Costle,* 561 F. 2d. 983 (D.C.Cir. 1977)]

This court opinion and others firmly established that when sexual harassment causes a job detriment, it is *sex* discrimination because sex is present as a substantial factor for no legitimate reason. But what if a bisexual supervisor subjects both male and female employees to sexual harassment? While no courts have faced this case yet, some have opined that it would not be sex discrimination because men and women have both been treated equally, though distastefully.

Homosexual Harassment

Homosexual harassment has been recognized to be within the present legal theory of sexual harassment as sex discrimination. Let's look at two cases recently litigated in this area:

—A male worker in a youth services program charged that when he rejected the sexual advances of his male supervisor, he was fired. The Illinois federal district court determined that, while sexual harassment cases usually deal with demands made of females that would not be made of males, here the plaintiff presented an actionable legal claim—the "obverse of the coin," the court wrote—an alleged demand of a male employee that would not have been directed to a female. [*Wright v. Methodist Youth Services,* 25 FEP Cases 5656 (N.D. Ill. 1981)]

—A male shop mechanic alleged that when the plant manager made homosexual advances to him at a local restaurant, he refused and promptly complained to the president of the company. Although the manager denied the charges in the subsequent investigation, he was nevertheless warned that these allegations, if true, were a serious violation of company policy. Then the manager retaliated against the plaintiff because of his complaint by refusing to recall him to a position following an economic layoff. The Alabama federal district court found the employer liable for the sexual harassment because there was a "clear nexus" between the rejection of the sexual advances and the tangible job detriment. [*Joyner v. AAA Cooper Transportation,* 36 FEP Cases 1644 (M.D. Alabama, 1983)]

Other Legal Patterns

Another fact pattern that is emerging as illegal sexual harassment is when an employee brings an action for sexual harassment, even though she had previously yielded to the sexual demands. This cause of action was foreshadowed in the *Bundy v. Jackson* decision which held that an employee need not prove resistance to sexual overtures in order to have a Title VII claim. In *Vinson v. Taylor,* the same appellate court determined that it was hardly a major step for them to take from that point in *Bundy* to recognizing that a victim's "capitulation to on-the-job sexual advances cannot work a forfeiture of her opportunity for redress." In *Vinson,* the plaintiff was subjected to a barrage of demands to have sexual relations with her supervisor, some of which she agreed to because she feared she would be fired from her job. The court reasoned that an employee subjected to unwelcome sexual advances from another employee already faces a "cruel trilemma" in which she must choose between agreeing to the advances, opposing them or resigning from her job. It would be more "hideous," the court believed, to add a fourth option—"yielding and thereby losing all hope of legal redress for being put in this intolerable position in the first place." [36 FEP Cases 1423 (D. C. Cir. 1985)]

In its review of the *Vinson* case, the U.S. Supreme Court agreed with the appellate court that Vinson did not forfeit her Title VII claim because she was willing to participate in some of the sexual demands. The Supreme Court wrote: "The correct inquiry is whether (Vinson) by her conduct indicated that the alleged sexual advances were *unwelcomed,* not whether her actual participation in sexual intercourse was *voluntary.*" (Emphasis added.) [*Meritor Savings Bank, FSB. v. Mechelle Vinson,* 54 U.S. Law Week at 4706 (June 19, 1986).]

With a growth in the number of victims who will be asserting their rights and with the courts recognizing more legal causes of action, it is expedient that employers work diligently to combat sexual harassment in their workplaces. That prevention is the key is clear in the EEOC guidelines on sexual harassment which state:

> Prevention is the best tool for the elimination of sexual harassment. An employer should take all steps necessary to prevent sexual harassment from occurring, such as affirmatively raising the subject, expressing strong disapproval, developing appropriate sanctions, informing employees of their right to raise the issue of harassment under Title VII and developing methods to sensitize all concerned.

In short, the best advice is to BE SENSITIVE, BE RESPONSIVE and BE ACTIVE in your campaign to end sexual harassment in your workplace.

Appendix A

BLR Sexual Harassment Survey

A BLR Special Report

Sexual Harassment in the Workplace: What Are Employers Doing About It?

How big a problem is sexual harassment? What are employers doing to protect themselves and their employees?

We know our BLR readers are concerned about sexual harassment, and the legal experts rate it as one of the most difficult problems in today's workplace. To find out just what is happening, we've recently completed a survey of 157 organizations from across the country. We asked them about their policies, programs, and training, and we asked them for their suggestions.

You'll find a brief summary of the results below, followed by a detailed presentation of the data and the comments.

Results in Brief

• **Most organizations have policies.** Policies are in place at 78 percent of the organizations that participated in the survey. The message is clear: The organizations we surveyed have recognized the issue of sexual harassment and have made it part of their policy.

• **Printed materials are used to publicize the policies.** We found that 62 percent of the respondents went beyond writing the policy to actually distributing sexual harassment materials.

• **Top management is involved.** In over 70 percent of the organizations with a policy, top management had indicated its direct support of the sexual harassment policy.

• **Complaint procedures are in place.** Eighty-eight percent of respondents had complaint procedures in effect that could deal with sexual harassment complaints. In 36 percent of those cases, the procedures were specifically for sexual harassment complaints. Interestingly, nearly half of these complaint procedures had been in effect for three years or less. About 80 percent reported that the complaint procedures were either very effective or moderately effective.

• **Training programs are offered in many organizations.** Forty-three of our respondents offered special training on sexual harassment to employees.

• **Participants' suggestions and comments varied.** We recommend that you read through the comments and suggestions which are found at the end of this report; they are interesting and revealing, and we think that they will be helpful, also. One of the most interesting things is that the respondents seem to fall into one of two camps. The first group consists of those who are very worried and concerned. They say the situation should be treated very seriously. The second group appears to comprise those who have had no trouble so far. They say that the problem isn't so great and doesn't deserve special attention. We suspect that this latter group is in for a rude awakening.

SURVEY RESULTS IN DETAIL

You will find below an analysis of the results of the survey, question by question. The comments and suggestions of respondents are at the end of the survey.

One hundred fifty-seven organizations responded to the survey. The chart below presents demographic details of the respondents.

Appendix A—Survey

Profile of Respondents

Geographic Area		Number of Employees		Industry Group	
Eastern U.S.	18	1-99	29	Manufacturing	38
Southern U.S.	40	100-499	65	Nonmanufacturing business (finance/services)	51
East-central U.S.	41	500-999	20		
Western U.S.	31	999+	37	Nonbusiness (Healthcare/ Education/Government)	62
West-central U.S.	25				
No response	2		6		6

Basic Steps Employers Are Taking to Combat the Problem

The first charts show the basic activities employers have undertaken in response to the sexual harassment issue. In all cases, the charts will be given first for "geographic area," and then for "number of employees" and "industry group."

By geographic area:

	All	Eastern U.S.	Southern U.S.	East-central U.S.	Western U.S.	West-central U.S.
Percentage of employers who have						
Published a policy—	78%	83%	80%	76%	77%	76%
Established a complaint procedure—	88	78	85	93	90	88
Established a procedure just for sexual harassment complaints	36	44	33	34	42	32
Conducted awareness training	43	50	40	39	58	36

By number of employees:

	All	1-99	100-499	500-999	Over 999
Percentage of employers who have					
Published a policy—	78%	59%	85%	80%	81%
Established a complaint procedure—	88	69	91	95	92
Established a procedure just for sexual harassment complaints	36	28	49	30	22
Conducted awareness training	43	21	43	60	51

By industry group:

	All	Manufacturing	Nonmanufacturing business (finance services)	Nonbusiness (Healthcare/ Education/Government)
Percentage of employers who have				
Published a policy—	78%	76%	90%	69%
Established a complaint procedure—	88	92	86	85
Established a procedure just for sexual harassment complaints	36	42	31	34
Conducted awareness training	43	53	43	37

Do you have a policy regarding the prohibition of sexual harassment?

"Yes," responded 78% of those who participated in our survey. Policies were somewhat more prevalent in the East and South, and the smaller-sized organizations (1-99 employees) were less likely to have policies (59% versus 80% for the larger organizations).

Participants in nonmanufacturing industries were much more likely to have policies (90%) than were nonbusiness organizations (69%) and manufacturing organizations (76%).

Do you have a procedure whereby employees who feel they have been victims of sexual harassment can complain?

Complaint procedures were present in 88 percent of respondents' companies. Smaller organizations were less likely to have such a procedure, with only 69 percent, while the larger organizations had percents in the 90's.

Is this procedure specifically for sexual harassment?

Significantly, only 36% responded yes. In size, the mid-sized (100-499 employees) were most likely to have a specific policy, with almost half (49 percent) reporting.

Have you conducted training in your institution/company on sexual harassment?

Forty-three percent of respondents had conducted training. Such training was more common in the East (50 percent) and the West (58 percent), and larger organizations were more likely to offer it. Only 21 percent of smaller (1-99 employees) organizations offered training.

Primary Method of Disseminating Information

The next set of charts shows how organizations have handled the question of how to inform their employees about their policies.

By geographic area:

How has the policy been disseminated?	All	Eastern U.S.	Southern U.S.	East-central U.S.	Western U.S.	West-central U.S.
Meeting	8%	11%	5%	10%	10%	4%
Training	12	0	0	0	0	8
Management	12	6	3	0	0	0
Written materials	62	61	65	54	71	60
Contract	1	0	0	0	0	4
Other	6	6	8	12	3	0

By number of employees:

How has the policy been disseminated?	All	1-99	100-499	500-999	Over 999
Meeting	8	7	8	10	8
Training	1	0	3	0	0
Management	1	0	2	5	0
Written materials	62	41	69	60	62
Contract	1	0	2	0	0
Other	6	7	5	5	11

By industry group:

How has the policy been disseminated?	All	Manufacturing	Nonmanufacturing business (finance services)	Nonbusiness (Healthcare/Education/Government)
Meeting	8	13	12	2
Training	1	3	2	0
Management	1	3	0	2
Written materials	62	50	69	61
Contract	1	3	0	0
Other	6	8	6	6

How has the policy been disseminated in your company/institution?

Only those with policies responded to this question. Of those, 62 percent used written policies, posters, and other materials; and eight percent used the medium of meeting. (See chart above)

Interestingly, only 45 percent of small organizations had dissemination programs that involved written materials.

Top Management's Support Comes in the Form of:

The next charts show how top management has made known its support for sexual harassment policies.

Appendix A—Survey

By geographic area:

	All	Eastern U.S.	Southern U.S.	East-central U.S.	Western U.S.	West-central U.S.
How has top management indicated its support?						
Meetings	8	6	3	10	16	8
Adoption of policy	10	6	8	12	10	16
Endorsement	7	6	5	7	10	8
Seminars	3	11	3	0	6	0
Orientation	3	0	5	2	6	0
Investigation/ enforcement	11	17	5	10	19	12
Other	31	33	43	32	13	24

By number of employees:

	All	1-99	100-499	500-999	over 999
How has top management indicated its support?					
Meetings	8	7	15	5	0
Adoption of policy	10	7	9	15	14
Endorsement	7	7	9	5	5
Seminars	3	0	3	10	0
Orientation	3	0	2	0	11
Investigation/ enforcement	11	10	9	10	11
Other	31	24	29	35	35

By industry group:

	All	Manufacturing	Nonmanufacturing business (finance services)	Nonbusiness (Healthcare/ Education/Government)
How has top management indicated its support?				
Meetings	8	16	2	10
Adoption of policy	10	8	10	13

57

Endorsement	7	8	10	5
Seminars	3	3	4	2
Orientation	3	0	4	5
Investigation/ enforcement	11	8	14	6
Other	31	29	39	26

How has management shown its support?

Results to this question were hard to evaluate, since over thirty percent of the respondents indicated "other" as the type of support. However, in over 70 percent of the organizations with a policy, top management indicated its direct support of the sexual harassment policy. Of those that responded specifically, 11 percent indicated that support was shown by investigation and enforcement, ten percent by adoption of policy on harassment, eight percent by meetings, and seven percent by endorsement.

Length of Time Procedure Has Been in Effect

The next charts show the amount of time during which the procedures have been in effect in the organizations.

By geographic area:

	All	Eastern U.S.	Southern U.S.	East-central U.S.	Western U.S.	West-central U.S.
How long has this procedure been in effect?						
1-3 years	46	29	46	51	48	48
4-5 years	18	28	25	15	13	16
6-10 years	8	6	0	12	10	16
Over 10 years	5	0	6	10	6	0

By number of employees:

	All	1-99	100-499	500-999	Over 999
How long has this procedure been in effect?					
1-3 years	46	12	37	30	35
4-5 years	18	13	14	35	25
6-10 years	8	0	9	0	19
Over 10 years	5	6	5	10	3

Appendix A—Survey

By industry group:

	All	Manufacturing	Nonmanufacturing business (finance services)	Nonbusiness (Healthcare/Education/Government)
How long has this procedure been in effect?				
1-3 years	46	45	43	48
4-5 years	18	23	18	16
6-10 years	8	8	14	5
Over 10 years	5	8	0	8

How long has this procedure been in effect?

Forty-six percent of respondents said that their procedures had been in effect three years or less. Only five percent had had procedures for over ten years. Larger organizations tended to have had policies in effect longer.

Effectiveness of Procedure

The next question focuses on whether the procedures in the previous question were judged to be effective.

By geographic area:

	All	Eastern U.S.	Southern U.S.	East-central U.S.	Western U.S.	West-central U.S.
Has this procedure been effective?						
Very effective	46	33	50	37	61	44
Moderately effective	32	39	23	44	26	32
Not effective	2	0	0	0	3	8

By number of employees:

	All	1-99	100-499	500-999	Over 999
Has this procedure been effective?					
Very effective	46	38	43	60	46
Moderately effective	32	21	35	25	41
Not effective	2	0	3	0	3

By industry group:

	All	Manufacturing	Nonmanufacturing business (finance services)	Nonbusiness (Healthcare/Education/Government)
Has this procedure been effective?				
Very effective	46	45	47	42
Moderately effective	32	42	27	32
Not effective	2	0	4	2

Has this procedure been effective?

Very effective replied 46 percent of respondents, while 32 percent said moderate, and two percent said the effect was not good. These programs seemed particularly effective in the midsize (500-999 employees) where 60 percent said they were very effective.

Who Is Being Trained?

These charts show what levels and types of employees are trained by different organizations.

Note: percents add up to more than 100 due to the possibility of multiple answers.

By geographic area:

	All	Eastern U.S.	Southern U.S.	East-central U.S.	Western U.S.	West-central U.S.
Who has been trained?						
Top management	33	39	35	29	42	24
Middle management	40	44	35	41	48	32
Employee	13	17	8	15	19	12
First-line supervisor	38	39	35	41	39	36
Other, specify	4	11	10	2	0	0

By number of employees:

	All	1-99	100-499	500-999	Over 999
Who has been trained?					
Top management	33	17	35	40	38
Middle management	40	21	38	55	49
Employee	13	10	17	5	11

Appendix A—Survey

First-line supervisor	38	21	34	55	49
Other, specify	4	0	3	10	3

By industry group:

	All	Manufacturing	Nonmanufacturing business (finance services)	Nonbusiness (Healthcare/Education/Government)
Who has been trained?				
Top management	33	37	37	27
Middle management	40	50	41	32
Employee	13	16	14	10
First line supervisor	38	53	37	29
Other, specify	4	3	0	6

Who has been trained?

Top management was trained in 33 percent of responding firms offering training. Smaller firms and nonbusiness firms were less likely to offer training to top management.

Middle management employees were trained at 40 percent of responding organizations. Larger organizations were more likely to offer training, with 55 percent of companies with 500-999 employees reporting, and 49 percent of organizations with over 999 employees reporting.

First-line supervisors were trained at 38 percent of responding organizations

Other employees were trained at only 13 percent of responding organizations.

What Kinds of Materials Have Been Used in Training?

The charts that follow indicate the types of materials that organizations are using to present their policies and educate their employees.

Note: percents add up to more than 100 due to the possibility of multiple answers.

By geographic area:

	All	Eastern U.S.	Southern U.S.	East-central U.S.	Western U.S.	West-central U.S.
What kinds of materials have been presented in the training?						
Films	23	17	23	27	26	20
Written materials	33	44	30	29	42	24

| Lectures | 38 | 39 | 33 | 37 | 45 | 36 |
| Other, specify | 6 | 6 | 10 | 2 | 10 | 0 |

By number of employees:

	All	1-99	100-499	500-999	Over 999
What kinds of materials have been presented in the training?					
Films	23	7	17	35	35
Written materials	33	14	34	35	43
Lectures	38	14	35	60	43
Other, specify	6	7	0	10	11

By industry group:

	All	Manufacturing	Nonmanufacturing business (finance services)	Nonbusiness (Healthcare/ Education/Government)
What kinds of materials have been presented in the training?				
Films	23	32	18	19
Written materials	33	45	25	31
Lectures	38	42	37	32
Other, specify	6	3	6	6

What kinds of materials have been presented in the training?

Films were used by 23 percent of responding employers.

Written materials were used at 33 percent of organizations responding.

Lectures were used by 38 percent of respondents.

COMMENTS OF PARTICIPANTS

Do you have any advice for other institutions/companies based on your experience with sexual harassment in the workplace?

One of the most interesting and informative parts of any survey is the collection of comments and suggestions that those returning the survey provide. While we can't list every comment, we have collected here those that we think are most representative and will be most helpful.

Brief Suggestions

Publicize the policy and enforce it.
Central U.S. publisher

Take care of the situation immediately.
Central U.S. hospital

Advise having a policy.
Central U.S. human services agency

Act immediately—investigate and discipline.
Southern restaurant chain

Use your policy.
Central U.S. hospital

Act quickly to resolve problem.
Southern manufacturer

Treat all employees equally.
Eastern manufacturer

Inform supervisors and managers.
Southern state agency

Confront the issue!
Central U.S. wholesaler

Have complaint in writing and investigate all of them.
Southern hospital

Documentation is a key factor.
Southern utility

Move quickly—investigate thoroughly.
Southern utility

Talk to your supervisors—one-on-one.
Southern manufacturer

Be prepared.
Southern service organization

Respond with investigation without fail.
Eastern manufacturer

Investigate and Act

Yes, don't ignore even the slightest complaint—investigate ASAP!
Eastern manufacturer

Act promptly on complaint—let complainant know that action is being taken—investigate—be firm —be fair—don't go for overkill.
Central U. S. distribution center

Always take charges seriously—investigate thoroughly and get legal advice on proper handling.
Central U. S. real estate organization

Let the appropriate person know immediately. Do not wait or try to handle on own. It might be misinterpreted if allowed to continue for any period.
Western software company

Respond to all complaints quickly, seriously, and with as severe a set of consequences as appropriate and possible.
Western manufacturer

Once harassment is known, investigate thoroughly and take action immediately—do not hesitate.
Western newspaper

Get on with enforcement of the law! To delay will cause more problems for the organization.
Southern hospital

Deal with the problem the instant it becomes apparent and give feedback to the person filing the complaint. Then document your actions!
Western manufacturer

Investigate thoroughly and immediately and take corrective action when and if needed.
Western motel and casino

Take prompt action, document, take action even if can't prove guilt or innocence.
National innkeeper

Communication

Have all present and future employees read and sign a statement giving the company's view on sexual harassment.
Southern manufacturer

Policy and procedures should be strongly communicated through supervisory training.
Southern city government

Keep reminding employers and employees of the potential problems they face when unwelcome conduct is allowed.
Central U. S. educational institution

Educate your superiors; publish grievance procedure and develop and promulgate written policy.
Southern restaurant management company

Be sincere with communication that sexual harassment will not be tolerated and spell out the penalties.
Eastern publisher

Make sure all involved are aware of what may constitute sexual harassment and what the ramifications could be!
Western telecommunications company

Be sure to have a policy; communicate the policy on a regular basis; post as a permanent poster.
Central U. S. utility

Communicate to all employees the possible liability to both the company and the employee.
Western savings and loan

Make the policy. Also verbalize to the employees. This lets the employees know the policy will be followed.
Central U. S. utility

More women should be made aware of their rights.
Central U. S. city government

Make employees aware that both men and women can be victims of sexual harassment as well as the perpetrator.
Central U. S. residential care center

Maintain open-door policy. Keep in touch with what's happening in the workforce (grapevine).
Eastern manufacturer

Have a strict written policy and reporting procedure. Re-inform all employees regarding policy every year.
Central U. S. manufacturer

Be open and honest in dealing with situations and/or complaints.
Central U. S. manufacturer

Recognize the possible existence of it and be very firm in your statement of unacceptability!
Central U. S. bank

Get formal outside instruction. Require all to attend. Have local top executive attend first session.
Central U. S. manufacturer

Training needs to be carried out on an ongoing basis. Address issue in supervisory training programs; publish antisexual harassment policies in employee handbooks. Employees must change their attitudes and stop trivializing the problem. Outline steps employees can take to fight on-the-job sexual harassment and inform victims of their legal rights when confronted with the problem.
Western manufacturer

Don't Overreact

Treat it as any other action; place emphasis where and when required; don't make it a separate issue even in training but include it with other items of like importance. Whether or not it exists should already be known to supervisors; however, if it isn't a problem, for sure it will be if it's overemphasized! Like anything else, if it exists, make sure corrective action is taken. Discipline all involved—management as well as hourly.
Midwest manufacturer

Best not to overreact to this issue. By issuing special policies, complaint procedures, etc. Resolve instances of harassment the same way you resolve other problems.
Eastern manufacturer

Monitor closely but don't overreact and make a bigger deal than it is.
Western hospital

Do not overreact but use a good investigative procedure before action. Do not try to ignore or cover up.
Southern bakery

As with most controversial subjects, we take care of any complaint properly, but do not publicize.
Southern state agency

Deal with it in terms of "inappropriate managerial behavior" or (peers) misconduct rather than single out as sexual harassment.
Western university organization

Should be directed towards harassment in general, as all forms (sexual, racial, etc.) of harassment are detrimental to both the interests of the employee *and* employer.
Central U.S. retailer

Other comments
Do not take this issue lightly; it's a serious issue to many women. At the same time, investigate all charges thoroughly; most women won't make such charges if they aren't valid, but there are exceptions. Education is very important—some men think they're "only teasing" and find it hard to understand why women take offense to what they (the men) almost consider to be compliments. Such men are dolts, but deserve at least an explanation and one chance to clean up their act.
Western manufacturer

Difficult to get harassee to actually complain, poor work results and the causes are never known.
Central U.S. manufacturer

Choose your management people very carefully and make sure they understand company policy and consequences if policy is not adhered to.
Southern hospital

Employ people with high moral standards and you won't have many problems.
Western manufacturer

1. Prevention is the best tool. 2. There are more cases in the work area than employee/employer can possibly imagine. Employers are just beginning to assert rights or take action. Will become increasingly more visible problem. Listen carefully to what employees are saying.
Eastern health care organization

Appears to be more apparent in situations where older managers are present—younger managers are more cautious in this area.
Southern educational institution

Don't be hesitant in addressing allegations of sexual harassment as soon as they arise. Postponing action can lead to future legal difficulties.
Eastern retirement home

Be honest. If someone is guilty—no matter who—follow through as the policy calls for. Do not cover up. Be fair to everyone.
Southern educational institution

Management must maintain confidentiality and act decisively to correct problem up to and including termination of offending party.
Western government contractor—R&D

Not a Problem

A number of respondents indicated that they simply didn't have a problem. The responses below are typical.

We have not had a problem with sexual harassment.

We have had very little, if any, of this type of harassment during the past two years.

Have not had any problems—that we are aware of.

We have had no issues regarding this area at this point.

To date, this division has had no problem in this area. One or two charges have been made within the last several years, but they were quickly settled. I would say that they were more in the area of sexual "discrimination" instead of sexual "harassment."

We have had only two complaints. Hardly enough experience to give advice.

We have had few problems. Those we have had were dealt with according to policy.

No problem experienced to date.

We haven't had any problem with it to date.

We have had no experience with this problem.

Don't do it; treat everyone with respect and you won't have this problem. We have a program but we've never had to use it to defend ourselves. Everyone here is equal and is treated that way!

Appendix B

Sample Policies and Forms

Sample Policy # 1
Courtesy of a Texas-based Service Organization

	ACTION	EFFECTIVE DATE	POLICY PROCEDURE NUMBER	PAGE NUMBER
▄▄▄▄▄▄▄▄▄▄	NEW	08/25/80	032-1	1 OF 2
	SUPERCEDES			OF

SUBJECT:	SEXUAL HARASSMENT		
APPLICATION:	ALL EMPLOYEES	APPROVED	▄▄▄▄

I. PURPOSE
Sexual harassment, either physical or verbal, is a violation of the law. The intent of this policy is to clarify the company's position in matters relating to compliance, discovery, and remedy.

II. POLICY
It is the intent of the company to maintain a work place free of sexual harassment from any source, either supervisors or co-workers, and to discourage any instance of malicious accusation.

III. DEFINITION
Sexual harassment is any repeated or unwanted verbal or sexual advances, sexually explicit derogatory remarks, or statements made by someone in the work place which are offensive or objectionable to the recipient, or which cause the recipient discomfort or humiliation, or which interfere with job performance, and which can be reasonably determined to constitute unlawful behavior as follows:
  1. Submission to the conduct is either an explicit or implicit term or condition of employment; or,
  2. Submission to or rejection of the conduct is used as a basis for employment decisions affecting the recipient; or,
  3. The conduct has the purpose or effect of substantially interfering with work performance, or creating an intimidating, hostile or offensive work environment.

IV. RESPONSIBILITY
  A. The Employee
    1. To be certain beyond a reasonable doubt that harassment exists, and is clearly directed toward the person objecting. Whenever possible, witnesses or other substantiating information should be provided.
    2. Advise the offending individual that the conduct in question is offensive, and request that it be discontinued immediately.
    3. If the offending conduct continues, or recurs, an official complaint may be placed through the office of the personnel director, or through the office of the chief executive officer.

  B. The Company
    1. The complaint will be reduced to written form by the company officer handling the complaint.

	ACTION	EFFECTIVE DATE	POLICY PROCEDURE NUMBER	PAGE NUMBER
▓▓▓▓▓▓	NEW	08/25/80	032-1	2 OF 2
	SUPERCEDES			OF

SUBJECT:	SEXUAL HARASSMENT		
APPLICATION:	ALL EMPLOYEES	APPROVED	▓▓▓

    2. A conference will be scheduled within 5 working days, with the understanding that the most immediate time practical will be utilized. Employees participating in the conference may choose to be accompanied by a co-worker, if that is felt to be desirable.

    3. The company officer conducting the conference will make every reasonable effort to determine the facts pertinent to the complaint. If the complaint can be resolved to the satisfaction of all parties, the matter will be considered closed, pending further complaint or additional information. In cases of recurrent complaint, or in cases of flagrant unlawful behavior, additional sanctions shall be employed.

    4. The company will make every reasonable effort to insure that no retaliation occurs.

V. SANCTIONS

The company will engage all or any combination of the following sanctions to remedy instances of sexual harassment:
1. Conference
2. Transfer
3. Suspension
4. Termination

Sample Policy # 2
Courtesy of a Nationwide Retail Organization

HARASSMENT

Harassment of employees due to their age, ancestry, color, creed, marital status, medical condition, national origin, physical handicap, race, religion, or sex by fellow employees and non-employees is demeaning to both the victims and the Company; it can result in high turnover, absenteeism, low morale and productivity, and an uncomfortable atmosphere to work in. Therefore, the Company will not tolerate any such harassment of its employees and will take affirmative steps to stop it.

Sexual harassment is behavior that is unwelcome and personally offensive; it can consist of sexually oriented "kidding" or jokes, physical contact such as patting, pinching or purposely rubbing up against another's body, demands for sexual favors tied to promises of better treatment or threats concerning employment for refusal, discriminating against an employee for refusing to "give in", or granting favors to one who submits. Other harassment can be jokes, comments, or other personally offensive and unwelcome behavior based on a person's age, ancestry, color, creed, marital status, medical condition, national origin, physical handicap, race, or religion that results in the loss of tangible job benefits or creates a hostile, obnoxious, or intimidating work atmosphere.

If you think another employee is harassing you because of your age, ancestry, color, creed, marital status, medical condition, national origin, physical handicap, race, religion, or sex, tell him or her that you find such behavior offensive, that such behavior is against Company policy, and ask him or her to immediately stop that behavior. It is important to let your fellow employees know when you consider such behavior offensive, as the Company hires people from a wide variety of cultural and ethnic backgrounds, and that person may not realize he or she thinks is proper could be seen by others as offensive. If that employee continues to "pester" you, immediately contact your supervisor, in writing, about the problem. If you feel you cannot seek help from your supervisor, contact his or her supervisor or your district personnel office, in writing, for assistance.

If you see another employee being harassed because of his or her age, ancestry, color, creed, marital status, medical condition, national origin, physical handicap, race, religion, or sex, tell him or her that the Company has a policy prohibiting such behavior, that he or she can demand the other stop such behavior, and that he or she can contact his or her supervisor, in writing, for help.

If another employee tells you he or she finds your behavior offensive, do not get angry or insulted. People have different ethnical values and standards, and may be offended by behavior you think is proper. Tell the employee you did not realize he or she would be offended by your behavior and stop the complained of conduct.

If you are harassed by a non-employee, contact your supervisor, in writing, for help. The Company cannot control the offensive behavior of all non-employees, but it will try to remedy the situation if it can.

Upon being told of such possible harassment, supervisory employees are expected to take prompt effective action to determine whether harassment has or is taking place, and to stop such behavior where it does exist. Supervisory employees are to submit a written report, including statements from the employees involved and any other relevant documentation, reporting the incident and detailing what actions they took to the district personnel manager. Any supervisory employee who condones, participates in, or initiates such harassment will be severely disciplined, including possible demotion or termination. Any employee knowing of a supervisory employee abusing his or her official position by condoning, participating in, or initiating such harassment should inform a higher level supervisor or appropriate personnel official, in writing, so the Company can take action against that supervisory employee.

No employee will be disciplined or otherwise retaliated against for complaining about such harassment. It is important that you inform the Company about such harassment, as the Company cannot do anything to remedy the situation if it does not know it exists.

The Company plans to incorporate harassment awareness training in future managerial, supervisory, and employee orientation courses. A copy of this policy will be made available to all new employees.

I hereby acknowledge that I have read and understand the above.

_____
NAME (PLEASE PRINT)

_____
NAME (SIGNATURE)

_____   _____
WITNESS   DATE

78 4/83

Sample Policy # 3
Courtesy of a Large State University

POLICY STATEMENT ON DISCRIMINATION AND HARASSMENT INCLUDING SEXUAL HARASSMENT

It is the policy of ███████ University to provide an educational and employment environment free from all forms of intimidation, hostility, offensive behavior and discrimination, including sexual harassment. Such discrimination or harassment may take the form of unwarranted verbal or physical conduct, verbal or written derogatory or discriminatory statements, which may result in decisions affecting status, promotions, raises, favorable work assignments, recommendations, class assignments or grades. Such behavior, or tolerance of such behavior, on the part of an administrator, supervisor, faculty or staff member violates the policy of the University and may result in disciplinary action including termination. The conduct herein described is both contrary to University policy and contrary to Seventh-day Adventist Christian beliefs and practice and may be illegal under both state and federal law.

The United States Equal Employment Opportunity Commission has defined sexual harrassment as unwelcome sexual advances, requests for sexual favors, and other verbal or physical conduct of a sexual nature when (1) submission to such conduct is made either explicitly or implicitly a term or condition of an individual's employment; (2) submission to or rejection of such conduct by an individual is used as the basis for employment decisions affecting such individual; or (3) such conduct has the purpose or effect of unreasonably interfering with an individual's work performance or creating an intimidating, hostile, or offensive working environment.

The State of ███████ has defined sexual harassment as unwelcome sexual advances, requests for sexual favors, and other verbal or physical conduct or communication of a sexual nature when (1) submission to such conduct or communication is made a term or condition either explicitly or implicitly to obtain employment, public accommodations or public services, education, or housing; (2) submission to or rejection of such conduct or communication by an individual is used as a factor in decisions affecting such individual's employment, public accommodations or public services, education, or housing; (3) such conduct or communication has the purpose or effect of substantially interfering with an individual's employment, public accommodations or public services, education, or housing, or creating an intimidating, hostile, or offensive employment, public accommodations, public services, educational, or housing environment.

An employee (including a student employee) who believes that he or she has been subject to discrimination or harassment should report the conduct to his or her immediate supervisor, and in the event the supervisor is the aggrieving party, to the next higher responsible party. If necessary, the employee grievance procedure should be utilized.

A student who believes that he or she has been discriminated against or harassed should report the conduct to the chairman of the department to which the teacher is assigned, and if the chairman is the aggrieving party, to the dean of the college/school in which he or she is enrolled.

Adopted by the Board of Trustees   August 12, 1985

Sample Policy # 4
Courtesy of a Major Foods Organization

POLICY STATEMENT

It is the policy of ███████, Inc. to prohibit any harassment of, or reluctance to train employees because of their sex.

Any employee who feels that he or she is experiencing harassment on the job because of his or her sex, or who feels that he or she is experiencing sex discrimination in receiving training, should be aware that the following procedures are available and should be utilized.

1. Any employee should immediately report all matters directly to the Personnel Manager.

2. The Personnel Manager will take immediate action to investigate any and all complaints registered.

3. Following the investigation of the complaint, the Personnel Manager shall review the facts and results of the investigation with the Bakery Manager and with the other appropriate members of Management and decide upon the validity of the complaint and determine how the complaint should be resolved.

4. If it is determined that an employee has engaged in harassment or reluctance to train, the Bakery will take immediate and appropriate remedial action, the nature of which will depend upon the severity of the determined offense.

5. After an investigation and determination of the merits of any complaint registered with the Personnel Manager, the Personnel Manager will meet with the complaining employee to discuss the results of the investigation. If the employee is dissatisfied with the processing of the complaint, the decision reached or the remedial action taken, if any, the employee will be afforded the opportunity to submit a written statement of his or her position for inclusion in his or her personnel file.

6. Any personnel found to have engaged in retaliation against an employee who has registered a complaint under this procedure or retaliation against any employee for assisting in the investigation of any registered complaint will be subject to immediate disciplinary action up to and including discharge.

Sample Policy # 5
Courtesy of a Pennsylvania Utility

▬▬▬▬▬▬▬▬ **Company**

POLICY AND PROCEDURE MANUAL

Department: ADMINISTRATION	Sub-Dept.: HUMAN RESOURCES EEO/AFFIRMATIVE ACTION	Authorized by: VICE PRESIDENT OPERATIONS
Subject: SEXUAL HARASSMENT		Date: 11/03/81
		Page: 401

1. **PREFACE**

   Legal and moral precepts make sexual harassment in the workplace, like harassment on the basis of color, race, religion or national origin in the workplace, completely improper. The Equal Employment Opportunities Commission has amended its guidelines on employment discrimination to add a specific section on sexual harassment (29CFR 1604, April 11, 1980). The Company's policy has long been to disapprove such discrimination and this policy is written to affirm the Company's position against sexual harassment.

2. **POLICY**

   2.1 It has long been the Company's policy that all employees have the right to work in an environment free from any type of unlawful discrimination, which includes an environment free from sexual harassment.

   Our policy on the subject is as follows:

   2.1.1 The Company shall not tolerate sexual harassment of employees in any form. Any such conduct shall result in disciplinary action up to and including dismissal.

   2.1.2 No supervisor shall threaten, suggest or imply that an employee's refusal to submit to sexual advances will adversely affect the employee's employment, evaluation, wages, advancement, assigned duties, shifts, or any other condition of employment or career development. Nor shall any supervisor suggest or imply that an employee's acquiescence to sexual advances may favorably affect the employee's condition of employment or career development.

   2.1.3 Other sexually-harassing conduct in the workplace, whether committed by supervisory or non-supervisory personnel, is also prohibited. This includes but is not limited to: offensive sexual flirtations, advances, propositions; verbal abuse of a sexual nature; graphic verbal commentaries about an individual's body; sexually degrading words used to describe an individual; and any offensive display in the workplace of sexually suggestive objects or pictures.

   2.2 Employees who believe they are being subjected to sexual harassment should inform appropriate supervisory personnel or the Human Resources Department.

Effective Pages:

401-403

Revision Date:
11/03/81

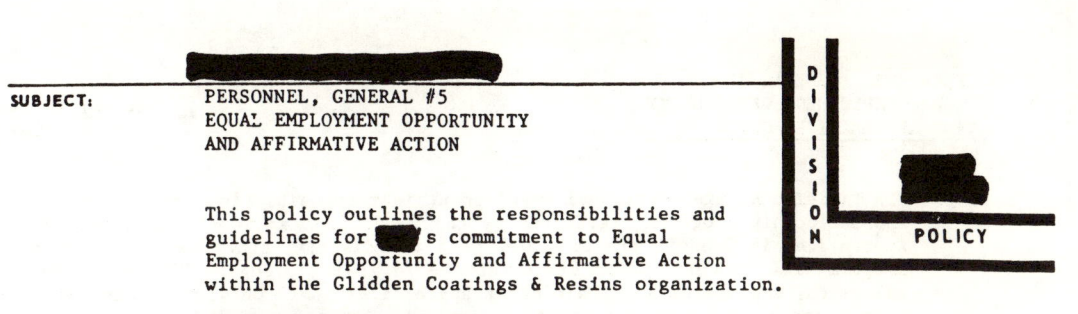

Sample Policy # 6
Courtesy of an Ohio-based Manufacturing Organization

SUBJECT: PERSONNEL, GENERAL #5
EQUAL EMPLOYMENT OPPORTUNITY
AND AFFIRMATIVE ACTION

DIVISION POLICY

This policy outlines the responsibilities and guidelines for ▆▆'s commitment to Equal Employment Opportunity and Affirmative Action within the Glidden Coatings & Resins organization.

SUPERSEDES: ▆▆▆▆▆▆▆▆▆▆ Division Policy P1-5 **DATE:** October 1, 1984
(Number and Date) dated July 18, 1983. (No change in policy; change in President's signature.)

AMENDS: None.
(Number and Date)

APPLICABLE TO: U.S. operations, including subsidiaries and joint ventures.

1. The Division has established an Equal Employment policy to ensure that all recruitment, placement, compensation, training and promotions are non-discriminatory and are based upon individual merit, ability and performance. All personnel actions and conditions of employment are administered without regard to race, color, religion, national origin, age, sex or handicap.

2. In addition, affirmative action will be taken to increase opportunities for minority, handicapped and female applicants and employees, as well as for veterans of the Vietnam Era.

3. Company policy is also established to insure that work environment is free of all forms of harassment including sexual harassment, that is; physical sexual advances or intimidations, and uninvited or suggestive remarks. Harassment can also include uninvited direct or suggestive remarks about an individual's age, religion, race, or handicap. Any employee who feels that he or she has been, or is being harassed, can advise his or her immediate supervisor if appropriate, or the personnel manager or administrator at his or her location. Incidents of discrimination or harassment will be promptly and thoroughly investigated and pursuant to the investigation outcome, appropriate action may be taken, up to and including discharge of the harassing employee.

4. Each Division manager and supervisor is responsible for implementing company policy to ensure compliance with the Civil Rights Act of 1964, Executive Order 11246, as amended, the Department of Labor Revised Order No. 4, the Rehabilitation Act of 1973 and the Vietnam Era Veterans Readjustment Act of 1974. Implementation includes activities and practices designed to enhance understanding, acceptance and compliance with the intent and spirit of Equal Employment Opportunity, Affirmative Action and freedom from harassment.

5. Personnel managers and administrators at each location are responsible for reporting quarterly recruiting, employment and promotion statistics on ▆▆ Corporation forms 9598 and 1329. They will also prepare annually a revised Affirmative Action Plan for submission to the Division Manager-Personnel Development, Cleveland Headquarters.

/continued

PERSONNEL, GENERAL #5
EQUAL EMPLOYMENT OPPORTUNITY
AND AFFIRMATIVE ACTION

October 1, 1984
Page 2

6. The Division Manager-Personnel Development is responsible for ensuring that local apprenticeship programs registered by the U. S. Department of Labor or a State Apprenticeship Council are operated on a non-discriminatory basis. Each such program will include in its standards the following pledge: "The recruitment, selection, employment and training of apprentices shall be without discrimination because of race, color, religion, national origin, sex or handicap." Corporation takes affirmative action to provide equal opportunity for apprenticeships and operates the apprenticeship program as required under Title 29 of the Code of Federal Regulations, Part 30."

   a. Personnel managers or administrators at locations having an apprenticeship program with five or more apprentices are required to prepare or to revise annually an Affirmative Action Plan for its apprenticeship program.

   b. The plan will establish goals and timetables for minority and female apprentices wherever underutilization exists.

7. Questions concerning this policy should be referred to the Manager-Personnel Development or the Vice President-Employee Relations and Administration.

President

Distribution: Z 3, 5, 9, 14, 16, 18, 23, 26, 27, 28, 33, 39, 49, 50, 52 (C&R Mgmt.)
Including International and Sales Representatives

Sample Policy # 7
Courtesy of a Wisconsin Government Agency

☒ POLICY		NUMBER SEC 031
☒ PROCEDURE	SEXUAL HARASSMENT	DATE EFFECTIVE 01/28/82
☐ MEMO		PAGE 1 OF 1

SUBJECT: SEXUAL HARASSMENT

General Policy

Harassment on the basis of sex is a violation of Section 703 of Title VII. Sexual Harassment, either physical or verbal, is an unlawful employment practice and will not be tolerated within.

Definition

Sexual Harassment is defined as unwelcome sexual advances, requests for sexual favors, and other verbal or physical conduct of a sexual nature when:

1. Submission to such conduct is made either explicitly or implicitly a term or condition of an individual's employment.

2. Submission to or a rejection of such conduct by an individual is used as the basis for employment decisions affecting such individual; or

3. Such conduct has the purpose or effect of unreasonably interfering with an individual's work performance or creating an intimidating, hostile, or offensive working environment.

Procedure

1. Any concern which an employe may have related to this issue should be brought immediately, through channels or directly (as the situation dictates), to the attention of the division administrator. The right of an individual to raise such issues is protected under Section 703 of Title VII of the Civil Rights Act of 1964, as amended.

2. Any employe of the Department who engages in such prohibited behavior will be subject to disciplinary action.

Sample Form
Courtesy of a State College

WRITTEN COMPLAINT

STAFF MEMBER'S NAME _____ POSITION _____

DEPARTMENT _____ NAME OF SUPERVISOR _____

1. Oral Complaint discussed with supervisor on _____
   Answer received on _____ not satisfactory.
   No answer received within three (3) days.

2. Staff Member's statement of complaint (include facts, dates, policy or regulation involved, if any, and the remedy desired).

   _____
   _____
   _____
   _____
   _____
   _____
   _____
   _____
   _____

Staff Member's Signature _____ Date _____

Date Received by Division/Administrative Department Head _____

Division/Administrative Department Head's Decision _____

_____
_____
_____
_____
_____

Date Given to Staff Member _____

_____
Division/Administrative Department Heads Signature.

SUBJECT: COMPLAINT PROCEDURE

Date received by Complaint Review Committee _____

COMPLAINT REVIEW COMMITTEE'S decision:

_____
_____
_____
_____
_____
_____
_____
_____
_____
_____
_____
_____
_____
_____
_____
_____
_____
_____
_____
_____
_____
_____
_____
_____

Date Given to Staff Member _____

Signed by _____
Complaint Review Committee

Distribution: The original form, completed by the employee filing the complaint will be used for submission(s), recording of decision(s) and returned to the employee at each consecutive step, if applicable. The decision rendering authority will prepare one xerox copy for his own departmental file, one copy for the individual(s) who answered the complaint at a previous step(s), and one copy for the employee's personnel file in the Employee Relations Office.

Appendix C

Sexual Harassment Awareness Training

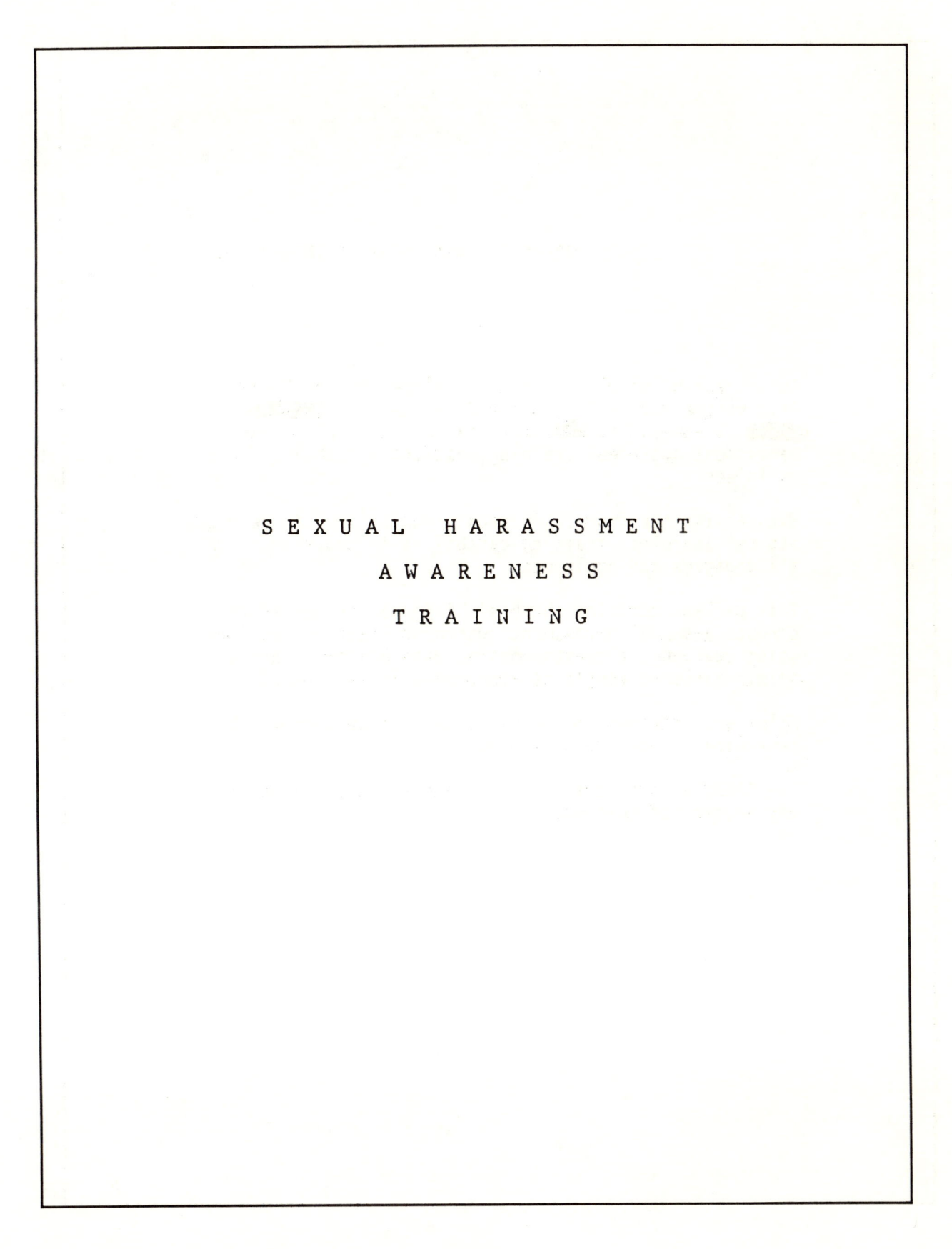

SEXUAL HARASSMENT
AWARENESS
TRAINING

SEXUAL HARASSMENT AWARENESS TRAINING

This training module has been developed by the Central Affirmative Action Programs Office (CAAPO), ███████ ███, as an aid to ███ organizations that plan sexual harassment awareness training sessions for their employees.

With assistance from CAAPO each organization can develop its own awareness training capability in order to reach all managers and employees.

This package contains the basic information needed to conduct a sexual harassment awareness training session using vugraphs, a questionnaire, case histories and a film. Workshop length is approximately two hours.

Films are retained in the CAAPO and can be borrowed by reserving in advance of the workshop.

The CAAPO is available for training and counseling on any segment of this module.

Sexual Harassment
Awareness Training Module
(2 Hours)

:05   Introduction

- Workshop Objectives

:15   • Exercise 1

             - Questionnaire
             - Discussion

:20   • Laws and Liability

             - EEOC Guidelines

- Types of Sexual Harassment

- Impact of Sexual Harassment

- Managers'/Supervisors' Responsibility

:35   • Film

:45   • Exercise 2

             - Case Histories
             - Small Groups Discussion
             - Large Groups Discussion

Note: If film is not used, workshop length can be reduced by approximately one-half hour.

Objectives:

1. To understand what sexual harassment is and what to do when it occurs.

2. To review company liability in regard to this issue.

3. To become more aware and sensitive to the issue of sexual harassment.

Preface your presentation (using copies of vugraphs attached, if desired) with the following information:

Sexual harassment is a form of sex discrimination and as such is illegal under Title VII of the Civil Rights Act of 1964.

Since the Equal Employment Opportunity Commission issued guidelines on sexual harassment in March 1980,   has established a company policy against harassment. Memos were issued by   in January 1981 to all employees and to division and group staff general managers stressing the importance of adhering to this policy, stating that any incidents of harassment would result in appropriate sanctions. He stated that managers would be responsible for monitoring this policy.

Copies of these memos are in the handouts, along with the complete text of EEOC guidelines, and   guidelines on what to do if you confront a situation of harassment, whether you are the Supervisor, the victim or an observer. Also includes guidelines on how to avoid being a harasser.

THE LAW

FEDERAL EEOC REGS. (MARCH, 1980):

"UNWELCOME SEXUAL ADVANCES, REQUESTS FOR SEXUAL FAVORS, OR OTHER VERBAL OR PHYSICAL CONDUCT OF A SEXUAL NATURE" ARE ILLEGAL WHEN:

- SUBMISSION IS A TERM OR CONDITION OF EMPLOYMENT

- SUBMISSION OR REJECTION IS USED AS BASIS FOR EMPLOYMENT DECISIONS

- SUCH CONDUCT INTERFERES WITH PERSON'S PERFORMANCE OR CREATES A "HOSTILE, INTIMIDATING, OR OFFENSIVE" WORK ENVIRONMENT.

2

TYPES OF SEXUAL HARASSMENT

TYPE	BEHAVIOR	HARASSER
POWER PLAYS	USING ONE'S POSITION OF AUTHORITY, EITHER IMPLICITLY OR EXPLICITLY, TO COERCE AN EMPLOYEE INTO COMPLYING WITH SEXUAL FAVORS.	MANAGER, SUPERVISOR
PHYSICAL	UNWANTED TOUCHING, FONDLING, PATTING, HUGGING, PINCHING, KISSING	SUPERVISOR, SUBORDINATE CO-WORKER

TYPES OF SEXUAL HARASSMENT

TYPE	BEHAVIOR	HARASSER
VERBAL	QUESTIONS AND COMMENTS ABOUT A PERSON'S SEXUAL BEHAVIOR, SEXUALLY ORIENTED JOKES, COMMENTS ABOUT A PERSON'S BODY, CONVERSATIONS FILLED WITH SEXUAL INNUENDO AND DOUBLE MEANINGS.	SUPERVISOR, SUBORDINATE, CO-WORKER
MENTAL/ NON-VERBAL	DISPLAYING SEXUALLY SUGGESTIVE PICTURES OR OBJECTS IN THE WORK-PLACE LEERING, OGLING IN A SEXUALLY DE-MEANING MANNER. GESTURING AND MAKING LEWD MOTIONS WITH ONE'S BODY.	SUPERVISOR, SUBORDINATE, CO-WORKER

4

IMPACT ON THE VICTIM	IMPACT ON THE ORGANIZATION
1. ECONOMIC	1. PRODUCTIVITY
2. JOB PERFORMANCE	2. MORALE
3. EMOTIONAL STRESS	3. JOB TURNOVER
4. PHYSICAL STRESS	4. LEGAL COSTS

MANAGEMENT'S/SUPERVISOR'S RESPONSIBILITY

- MAINTAIN A HARASSMENT-FREE WORK ENVIRONMENT

- KNOW THE COMPANY POLICY AND GUIDELINES

- COMMUNICATE THE POLICY AND YOUR POSITION RELATIVE TO HARASSMENT

- TAKE IMMEDIATE ACTION ON COMPLAINTS

PRESENTATION

Vugraph 1. THE LAW

Fed. EEOC Regs. (March, 1980):

"Unwelcome, etc."

1. Submission is a term or condition of employment.

    (Saying no to sexual advances can cost you your job)

2. Submission or rejection is used as basis for employment decisions.

    (Whether or not one is promoted is based upon whether one submits or agrees to the sexual favors requested.)

3. Such conduct interferes with person's performance or creates a "hostile, intimidating, or offensive" work environment.

    (Verbal or physical behavior of a sexual nature directed toward one which interferes with the job one is paid to do.)

Vugraphs 2 & 3. TYPES OF SEXUAL HARASSMENT

a) <u>Power Plays</u>

   (Can take the form of verbal abuse, physical contact, requests for sexual favors, e.g., propositions, or repeated requests for dates. Occurs between someone who has a position of power and his/her subordinate.)

b) <u>Physical</u>

   (Any physical conduct directed toward one that is unwelcome can constitute sexual harassment. This can vary from person to person and also from day to day: you may not mind it one day but be very offended by it the next. This behavior can occur between co-workers as well as between supervisor/subordinate.)

c) <u>Verbal</u>

(Sexually-oriented conversation, of whatever form, can cause problems for some people with the result that the workplace environment becomes stressful; interferes with productivity.)

d) <u>Mental/Non-verbal</u>

(Being the object of someone's staring or ogling; or of body language which is sexually suggestive. Working in an environment where material objects create an offensive environment and interferes with work.)

Vugraph 4. IMPACT ON THE VICTIM

1. <u>Economic</u>

If you lose your job because of sexual harassment (you were fired because you refused sexual advances, or you quit because it became intolerable) your financial situation can be greatly impacted, especially if you are out of work for a period of time.

2. <u>Job Performance</u>

While you may not lose your job if you refuse requests for sexual favors, you may find that your position is impacted in other ways: your performance reviews may deteriorate, parts of your job may be given to someone else; you may be transferred.

3 & 4. <u>Emotional and Physical Stress</u>

Studies have shown that victims of sexual harassment suffer the same kinds of emotional and physical stress that affect others when their jobs become stressful. Migranes, backaches are just a few of the affects of harassment.

Vugraph 4. IMPACT ON THE ORGANIZATION

1. <u>Productivity</u>

Any form of sexual harassment which causes a problem for the recipient of this kind of behavior interferes with work.

2. <u>Morale</u>

   Not only the morale of the victim is affected, but the morale of an entire office of people can be influenced by the act(s) of sexual harassment.

3. <u>Job Turnover</u>

   Replacing people costs money and time. Victims of sexual harassment eventually leave their positions whether they give the harassment as the reason or not. The Federal government estimates that it has cost the taxpayers $188M over a two-year period in job turnover, absenteeism and lost productivity because of unwanted sexual pressure.

4. <u>Legal Costs</u>

   The money being paid out to victims of sexual harassment continues to grow. Some examples of court cases and the cost to companies are as follows:

$100,000	Johns-Manville
$140,000	Ford Motor Co.
$ 52,000	Calif. Machine Shop
$196,500	Wisc. Dept. of Health & Services
$ 1,500	Five Managers of Western Electric were personally assessed $1500 each for harassing a woman.

   Vugraph 5.   MANAGERS'/SUPERVISORS' RESPONSIBILITY

- Maintain a harassment-free work environment.

   (Manage your department so that everyone is able to do their job without interference of any kind. This involves an awareness on your part of the climate that is prevalent in your work area.)

- Know the company policy and guidelines.

   (Refer to   memos of March 1981, subject "Harassment Policy" and to the EEOC Sexual Harassment Guidelines, March 1980.)

- Communicate the policy and your position relative to harassment.

   (Inform your employees of the company policy. Establish an open-door environment so that your employees will feel free to discuss any problems of employee misconduct with you.)

- Take immediate action on complaints.

    (When anyone comes to you and complains of sexual harrassment, take the complaint seriously and handle it with confidentiality. Speak to all parties involved. Consult with your Personnel Manager, if necessary.)

    (Refer to How to Handle a Sexual Harassment Complaint in handouts)

NOTE:

Points to Emphasize

- The Company is liable in cases of supervisor-subordinate sexual harassment whether they are aware of it or not.

- In cases of conduct between fellow employees, an employer is responsible for acts of sexual harassment where the employer knows or should have known of the conduct, <u>unless it can show that it took immediate and corrective action</u>.

- Violators of company policy on harassment will be disciplined; this could include suspension or termination, depending on the nature of the harassment.

EXERCISE 1

Questionnaire

Hand out copies of the questionnaire (attached) to the participants and give them five minutes to read it and decide if each situation could result in a case of sexual harassment.

Discussion.

All of the situations except numbers 1 and 5 have the potential for sexual harassment. One and five are examples of sex discrimination; since there is no implication of sexuality involved, it is not sexual harassment.

Numbers 2, 3, 4, 6, 7, and 9 have the potential for sexual harassment. The boss in number 2 needs to be sensitive to the question of whether any of the women he hugs objects to his behavior. This kind of conduct is best confined to social, not professional, situations.

Number 3: Asking an employee to have a meeting after work is all right if there are no implied sexual overtones. Better still, have the meeting in the office.

Number 4 is definitely an example of sexual harassment: using one's position of authority to gain sexual favors in return for improved job status. This is "third party" sexual harassment. In this case either one of the two women who didn't get the job could file a case against the company.

Numbers 6, 7, and 9 involve behavior which, under the law, creates an environment that could be considered "intimidating and hostile", therefore illegal.

Number 8 is the only one that is not discriminatory on the face of it. The point to be made here is that emphasis should be placed on the professional work performed and not on a person's appearance.

QUESTIONNAIRE

Sexual Harassment Workshop

Read the following and decide if each situation illustrated represents a potential case of sexual harassment in the workplace. CIRCLE ONE ANSWER.

<u>Sexual Harassment</u>?

1. At a business meeting of his professional staff the lab manager asks the only woman engineer present to serve the coffee. yes   no   don't know

2. Every morning the boss comes in and hugs all the women in the office. He says "I'm just a very affectionate person". yes   no   don't know

3. Sharon's boss asks her to join him for a drink after work to discuss her new job assignment. yes   no   don't know

4. Shirley's boss offers her a promotion if she'll go out with him. She accepts and as a result receives the promotion she and two other women in the office were vying for. yes   no   don't know

5. Jane applied for a job that required extensive travel. She was turned down because the out-of-town trips required her to travel with two male employees. yes   no   don't know

6. One of the secretaries in Bob's office put up the center-fold picture from Playgirl magazine. The nude male picture displayed on the wall disturbs Bob whenever he looks at it. yes   no   don't know

7. Everyone in James' deparment is often involved in verbal joking behavior with sexual overtones. The new budget analyst objects and asks for a transfer. yes   no   don't know

8. Laura's co-worker John remarks how pretty she looks today in her new dress. yes   no   don't know

9. The saleswoman who visits the purchasing agent on her regular call constantly addresses the male receptionist as "honey" and stares at his tight-fitting pants. yes   no   don't know

EXERCISE 2

CASE HISTORIES

The case histories on the following pages are based on actual cases of sexual harassment

Implementation

Depending on the size of the group, divide the participants into five small groups of three or four, distributing copies of the five case histories among them. (Retain "Resolutions") Allow ten minutes for each small group to discuss their case history and decide the proper action to be taken. Reconvene to a large group. Each small group shares their case history and their solution/discussion with the entire group.

Depending on the time allotted for the workshop, you may want to use less than five case histories.

Use the "Resolutions" as your backup information on the outcome of the cases.

Case #1

Samantha worked as a secretary to Henry Wolf, a Senior Accountant, for one year. Henry often invited her out after work to join him for cocktails. She refused his offers gently but firmly until time for her performance review. He told her the only time he would have to give her her review was after work. He said it might as well be over cocktails as in the office, so she agreed. He told her that her work was coming along very nicely and that he had no complaints and would put in a nice increase for her. He then asked her if she would mind if he dropped over to her apartment for a nightcap after he finished some work at the office. Samantha said she did not believe this to be proper knowing that Mr. Wolf was married. Mr. Wolf assured her that his wife was understanding. She still refused his offer, and said that she was very tired and would be retiring early. Henry then said, if she was more cooperative he could see that she was soon reclassified to a higher level secretary since he was entitled to an Executive Secretary.

Samantha said she would very much appreciate that if he felt she was qualified, but that she was not interested in a promotion if it was conditioned upon her being "cooperative". Henry said she might be sorry for that attitude.

Later when Samantha received her increase, she found it to be a minimum amount. She asked Mr. Wolf why her increase was so little after he had told her her performance was satisfactory. He told her that since he had talked with her, her performance had deteriorated. Samantha told Mr. Wolf that she was going to file a grievance because she did not feel she had been treated fairly.

Did Samantha have justifiable reasons for a grievance? Should Mr. Wolf have been concerned regarding his legal liability and responsibility? If Samantha came to you with this story, how would you have handled it?

Case #2

Tom Reynolds works as a Personnel Manager for an electronics firm.

Tom received a call one day from George Lange who said he was the husband of Marianne who worked for the company. George called, he said, to complain about the harrassment Marianne was receiving from her boss. He said Marianne told him that her boss would call her into his office, close the door, and ask her intimate details about her sex life, touch and fondle her and insist she go out with him. She has been afraid to complain for fear he would fire her, George said.

Tom said that until Marianne herself came in to see him and made a complaint, he could do nothing. After the call, Tom sat there wondering how he would handle the complaint if there should be one. The problem was, the accused harasser, Ben Booke, was one of their top level managers.

Marianne did come to Tom and repeated the story her husband had told to him. Tom said he would investigate. He arranged to meet with Ben, and in that meeting he told Ben of the accusations that had been made. Ben admitted they were true. He expressed surprise that so much had been made of it. Tom contacted two other women who had worked for Ben in the past. Separately, their stories correlated with Marianne's. All three said they had been the recipients of intimidating sexual advances. The previous two secretaries both stated they left their jobs because of his behavior.

Do you think Tom handled this matter properly? What action should the company take against Ben, if any?

Case #3

Janice started a new job as secretary in a large firm. After several weeks she went to Lois Miller, the Personnel Manager, and requested a transfer to another work area within the company.

At first Janice was reluctant to explain the reason for her request, saying only that she would rather work in another area. Finally, upon probing by Lois, she said that she was uncomfortable with the "joking" behavior in her office; that she found the comments which appeared to be acceptable to everyone else offensive to her.

Lois told Janice she would look into the matter.

Lois contacted several other women who worked in Janice's department and set up meetings with them. She explored with them the ways in which people interacted with each other in their office, alluding to Janice's comments.

The women acknowledged that the interaction between co-workers was very informal and yes, there was a lot of joking which had sexual overtones. But they said, that's always the way it has been since they worked there.

Do you have any problems with that?, Lois asked. Hesitant at first, the women finally admitted that they didn't like it much but had accepted it without comment.

A meeting later with a few men in the same department revealed that although they went along with the joking behavior, they, too, were not always comfortable with it.

How would you as a supervisor handle a situation like this if it occurred in your work area?

If the kind of environment described above is acceptable to all employees of the office except one, what would you do about that person's complaint?

Case #4

Anne worked as an accountant in a busy office of an aerospace firm. Within her immediate working area were six people including the supervisor. Anne was one of three women; the other two were secretaries. The remaining two men were also accountants.

Ann had been working with this group for several months when she complained to her supervisor that one of her male co-workers, Jim, was exhibiting a behavior toward her which was becoming very stressful. When questioned, she said that on several occasions she passed Jim in the hall and he pinched her. She said the first time it happened she expressed surprise and told him she was very upset at his behavior. However, she said, on several other chance meetings, the same incident occurred. That was when, Anne said, she decided to speak to her supervisor. She said she wasn't going to put up with it and what was her supervisor going to do to stop it? Her supervisor said he would speak to Jim.

When confronted with the accusation, Jim denied that any such incidents had taken place. "She's crazy", he said, "I never touched her".

The supervisor relayed this information to Anne saying that under the circumstances since there were no witnesses, there was nothing he could do. It was one person's word against another. Anne, furious, went to the Personnel Manager and told him her story. An investigation by the Personnel Manager produced the same results. Anne refused to remain in the area any longer and with the help of Personnel, found another position in the company and transferred.

What would you do as a supervisor if you were faced with this problem? How would you discern the truth? Is there a fair solution for all?

105

Case #5

Jeanne, a computer operator, often had to work late because of severe understaffing in her area. A night shift service worker, Ed, would frequently stop by to have a friendly chat with Jeanne. At first Jeanne felt rather secure knowing Ed was around and she was not alone in the building. As she continued to work at night, however, Ed's visits became more and more frequent and he became increasingly familiar, to the point where Jeanne finally had to tell him to stop bothering her. Ed was not deterred by her protestations and continued to find reasons for stopping by and talking with her or telephoning her. He started making overtures to her and asked her if she would have an affair with him. She became frightened at his persistence and what he might do if she kept resisting his advances.

Jeanne decided to report the situation to her supervisor, Frank, who advised her to just ignore the man and if he continued to bother her, to call him at home and he would come in and reprimand him.

When she ignored Ed, he accidentally turned the lights out on her one night, and another night jokingly told her he was going to have all the janitors waiting for her when she left the building.

She reported these incidents to Frank, who reported them to his manager, John. They told her to work at home whenever possible rather than working late at the office.

However, it was not always possible to do her work at home. During the evenings Jeanne worked, the attention from Ed continued.

Jeanne went to see her Personnel Manager, who spoke with Ed's supervisor. The supervisor reprimanded Ed and told him never to speak to Jeanne again. Ed was subsequently transferred to another building.

Do you think Ed's actions constituted sexual harassment? What action would you as a supervisor take if Jeanne complained to you? Was the punishment proper?

RESOLUTION

CASE #1

This is a clear case of sexual harassment, where an employment decision (a promotion) was based upon the response to a request for sexual favors.

The company is held "responsible for the actions of its supervisors with respect to sexual harassment regardless of whether the specific acts complained of were authorized or even forbidden by the employer and regardless of whether the employer knew or should have known of their occurrence".

EEOC Guidelines on Discrimination Because of Sex, 1980.

RESOLUTION

CASE #2

The Personnel Manager met with the senior manager who admitted to the allegations. He seemed not to understand or acknowledge the seriousness of his actions. He was terminated. The decision was based on the fact that the conduct had occurred overtime and that several women had been involved.

(It appeared that there were still other women who had worked for Ben and been recipients of his behavior who were not brought into the case.)

RESOLUTION

CASE #3

In this case the Personnel Manager met with the Department Manager and shared her findings with him. A meeting with all employees in the department was held in which the company policy on sexual harassment was reiterated and discussed. The outcome was that Janice agreed to remain with her department.

It is important that any individual complaint be seriously investigated regardless if it conflicts with the conduct of the majority. Transferring someone out of a department as a solution without working the problem is forfeiting management responsibility and could place the company in legal jeopardy if a complaint is filed.

RESOLUTION

CASE #4

Anne's transfer was requested by her and resolved the problem. It is important that a resolution which removes the victim to another area be voluntarily complied with or we could have a case of retaliation (a no-win situation).

If both parties involved are in disagreement as to what occurred, often a meeting with both and a restatement of company policy will difuse the situation.

RESOLUTION

CASE #5

This is a case of sexual harassment, since the behavior directed toward Jeanne was perceived as harassing and caused her extreme distress. Productivity was affected.

The escalation of this problem might have been avoided if action by Jeanne's management had been taken after the first complaint.

Whenever there is any doubt about how to handle a complaint of harassment contact your Personnel Manager immediately for assistance, particularly if (as in this case) the harasser fell outside the supervisor's jurisdiction.

FILMS ON THE SEXUAL HARASSMENT ISSUES

These particular films are maintained in the AAP Office and may be used for training purposes if so desired. If you wish to reserve one, please call

Contact Audio-Visual Services for projection scheduling

"The Work Place Hustle" 16mm

Color   30 Minutes

This film is designed to inform, motivate and sensitize the viewer to the damaging effects of sexual harassment. Contains a case history, skits, and separate male and female discussion groups.

"Preventing Sexual Harassment" 16mm

Color   25 Minutes

Dramatizes major points of the EEOC guidelines on sexual harassment through scenes acted out based on actual cases.

"The Power Pinch" 16mm

Color   25 Minutes

Narrated by Ken Howard, gives examples of sexual harassment through the use of scenarios and discussions.

THE SUPERVISOR:

HOW TO HANDLE A SEXUAL HARASSMENT COMPLAINT

o In confidence, determine the nature of the harassment, when and where it occurred; what the victim's response was; and if there were any witnesses.

o Investigate the complaint or ask your Personnel Manager for assistance.

o An investigation should include:

   a. Talking with the accused harasser regarding the complaint.

   b. Talking with witnesses, if any.

o If accused admits harassment, take appropriate action to prevent any reoccurrences. This action can take the form of:

   a. A discussion with the harasser regarding appropriate work behavior, and the consequences of non-compliance, including possible termination.

   b. Suspension or termination, depending upon the seriousness of the harassment.

o If the accused denies the harassment and there were no witnesses to verify the complaint, the supervisor should restate company policy to both parties and the expectations of proper work behavior.

o Document all discussions and actions taken.

o Seek assistance from your Personnel Manager.

THE VICTIM:

o   If unwanted behavior by another employee is directed toward you, take the following action:

   a.   Speak to the offender about his/her behavior. State firmly that you do not like it.

   b.   If the behavior persists, speak to your supervisor.

   c.   If the offender is your supervisor and he/she continues to harass you, speak to his/her superior, or see your Personnel Manager.

   d.   Document the incidents of sexual harassment: where and when it happened, who was present, and what happened.

HARASSER - HOW TO AVOID BEING LABELED AS

1. Anyone may be considered a harasser if their behavior towards another becomes unwanted, offensive, hostile or creates an offensive and disruptive work environment. Unwanted sexual behavior can apply in cases of supervisor to subordinate or among peers and is not limited to men/women situations.

2. The assumption that our behavior is acceptable to everyone with whom we come in contact creates a difficult situation for both the victim as well as the harasser. Whether harassment is intended or unintended, you may be appropriately accused of harassment if you indulge in such actions as:

    o Making sexual comments about a person's clothing or body.

    o Telling sexual jokes; using sexual innuendoes.

    o Touching, hugging, patting, kissing.

    o Repeated, unwanted overtures of a sexual nature.

    o Displaying lewd or offensive pictures or objects.

    o Using lewd or offensive gestures.

3. If you are a supervisor, your subordinates may not feel comfortable in telling you when they are offended or harassed. The attitude you exhibit towards your employees determines whether they find it easy or difficult to speak up regarding their treatment.

4. Be aware of how people respond to what you do and say. If an individual objects to your behavior towards them, listen and heed their objections. What is acceptable behavior to some people is not always acceptable behavior to others.

5. <u>Remember</u>: a complaint of sexual harassment can result in <u>a lawsuit</u> being filed against the company as well as the harasser.

Sexual Harassment: The Observor

1. Conduct in the workplace affects all who work there. Each of us has a responsibility not only to ourselves but to others to ensure that each individual's work performance is free of interference. Sexual harassment takes time and energy away from the task at hand.

2. If you are a supervisor and observe someone being sexually harassed, either verbally or physically, ask that person if such behavior bothers her/him. Don't assume that it is all right because the individual being harassed does not speak out.

3. If the victim expresses a negative attitude toward the behavior, as a supervisor you should speak to the harasser about his/her conduct.

4. If you are a co-worker who observes sexual harassment toward another, comment on it to the victim. Offer to support that individual if she/he wishes to complain to the supervisor or to the personnel department.

Appendix D

Federal Guidelines Regarding Sexual Harassment

Appendix D

Federal Guidelines Regarding Sexual Harassment

This Appendix contains the complete text of the Equal Employment Opportunity Commission's guidelines regarding sexual harassment. They appear in Title 29 of the Code of Federal Regulations, Section 1604.11 (29 CFR Sec. 1604.11).

§ 1604.11 Sexual harassment.

(a) Harassment on the basis of sex is a violation of Sec. 703 of Title VII.[1] Unwelcome sexual advances, requests for sexual favors, and other verbal or physical conduct of a sexual nature constitute sexual harassment when (1) submission to such conduct is made either explicitly or implicitly a term or condition of an individual's employment, (2) submission to or rejection of such conduct by an individual is used as the basis for employment decisions affecting such individual, or (3) such conduct has the purpose or effect of unreasonably interfering with an individual's work performance or creating an intimidating, hostile, or offensive working environment.

(b) In determining whether alleged conduct constitutes sexual harassment, the Commission will look at the record as a whole and at the totality of the circumstances, such as the nature of the sexual advances and the context in which the alleged incidents occurred. The determination of the legality of a particular action will be made from the facts, on a case by case basis.

(c) Applying general Title VII principles, an employer, employment agency, joint apprenticeship committee or labor organization (hereinafter collectively referred to as "employer") is responsible for its acts and those of its agents and supervisory employees with respect to sexual harassment regardless of whether the specific acts complained of were authorized or even forbidden by the employer and regardless of whether the employer knew or should have known of their occurrence. The Commission will examine the circumstances of the particular employment relationship and the job junctions performed by the individual in determining whether an individual acts in either a supervisory or agency capacity.

(d) With respect to conduct between fellow employees, an employer is responsible for acts of sexual harassment in the workplace where the employer (or its agents or supervisory employees) knows or should have known of the conduct, unless it can show that it took immediate and appropriate corrective action.

(e) An employer may also be responsible for the acts of non-employees, with respect to sexual harassment of employees in the workplace, where the employer (or its agents or supervisory employees) knows or should have known of the conduct and fails to take immediate and appropriate corrective action. In reviewing these cases the Commission will consider the extent of the employer's control and any other legal responsibility which the employer may have with respect to the conduct of such non-employees.

(f) Prevention is the best tool for the elimination of sexual harassment. An employer should take all steps necessary to prevent sexual harassment from occurring, such as affirmatively raising the subject, expressing strong disapproval, developing appropriate sanctions, informing employees of their right to raise and how to raise the issue of harassment under Title VII, and developing methods to sensitize all concerned.

(g) Other related practices: Where employment opportunities or benefits are granted because of an individual's submission to the employer's sexual advances or requests for sexual favors, the employer may be held liable for unlawful sex discrimination against other persons who were qualified for but denied that employment opportunity or benefit.

(Title VII, Pub. L. 88-352, 78 Stat. 253 (42 U.S.C. 2000e et seq.))
[45 FR 74677, Nov. 10, 1980]

---

[1] The principles involved here continue to apply to race, color, religion or national origin.

KF 228 .O64 1986